# THE
# GOSPEL

ACCORDING TO

# THE
# FIX

# AN INSIDER'S

# GUIDE TO

# A LESS

# THAN HOLY

# WORLD OF

# POLITICS

# THE
# GOSPEL

## ACCORDING TO

# THE
# FIX

### CHRIS CILLIZZA

BROADWAY BOOKS · NEW YORK

Published in the United States by Broadway Books, an imprint of the
Crown Publishing Group, a division of Random House, Inc., New York.

www.crownpublishing.com

BROADWAY BOOKS and the Broadway Books colophon are trademarks
of Random House, Inc.

Library of Congress Cataloging-in-Publication Data
Cillizza, Chris (Christopher Michael), 1976–
The gospel according to the fix / by Chris Cillizza.—1st ed.
      p.   cm.
  1. Elections—United States.   2. Political campaigns—
United States.   3. United States—Politics and government—2009–
            I. Title.
          JK1976.C54 2012
    324.973—dc23              2012011305

        ISBN 978-0-307-98709-9
        eISBN 978-0-307-98710-5

Printed in the United States of America

*Interior design by Maria Elias*
*Cover illustration © Fotosearch*
*Cover design by Kyle Kolker*

10  9  8  7  6  5  4  3  2  1

First Edition

To Gia
You are my sunshine

# CONTENTS

# THE
# GOSPEL

ACCORDING TO

# THE
# FIX

# INTRODUCTION

Politics takes itself very seriously. It shouldn't.
Yes, politics can be sublime. But it can also be ridiculous. Very ridiculous. I've spent the last decade covering campaign politics at the
so-close-to-the-picture-I-am-getting-a-headache level and, in that time,
have seen a Republican governor turn "hiking the Appalachian Trail"
into a euphemism for an extramarital affair, a congressman—and
aspiring mayor of New York City—accidentally post a picture of
his junk on his Twitter feed, and a North Carolina senator (and would-
be president) lie about, then admit to fathering, an out-of-wedlock
child.

I've also stood three hundred feet from the historic inauguration
of Barack Obama as the country's first black president (my god was
it cold that day), gone without sleep as the country tried to decide
who had won Florida—and the presidency—in 2000, and reported
on the attempted assassination of Arizona's congresswoman Gabrielle
Giffords.

I've also driven through the snow-covered streets of Des Moines
more times than I care to remember—and even got my rental car
stolen in downtown Des Moines once!—spent untold sums on the
Dunkin' Donuts in the Manchester, New Hampshire, airport, and
eaten barbecue by the pound, literally, in South Carolina.

I've done all of this in service of my stomach, er, blog—The
Fix—which began in 2005 and has been with me (in a good way)
every day since. My goal from the very first post until today has always

been the same: to serve as a tour guide for people through the increasing cacophony that is the political world. I am the Kenneth the Page—without the southern accent or hokey southern-isms—of the political world.

Every time I talk to people who either cover politics as their job or follow it as their hobby, I hear the same thing: there's too much news. It's impossible to keep up. My job is to keep up for you. To be the guy who obsessively checks his iPhone (hip!) at 2 AM, monitors his Twitter feed while feeding his infant son dinner (guilty), and would rather watch cable chat shows than *Two and a Half Men*. (Do people really watch that show?) I am the keeper of the political flame.

The fun of The Fix is that people pay me—thank you Don Graham and the *Washington Post*!—for doing just that. But I've always wanted to go longer, think bigger, use even MORE parentheses—to bring the love and passion I have for politics to more people who would love it if they only got to know it a little bit. (That line, by the way, was my [un]successful argument to my [unrequited] high school love.)

That's where the idea for *The Gospel* was born. To take what I loved about The Fix and make it bigger and better—kind of like Coke and New Coke. Wait . . .

Anyway, I hope this book radiates the joy I get from covering the political world in all its seriousness and silliness—hopefully both in equal measure. Politics is the greatest sport in the world with the highest stakes for those willing to play the game. I have been lucky enough to sit in the stands for the last decade. This book is my attempt to show you what I have seen.

# AMES STRAW POLL

## (Born August 1979, Died 8/13/2011)

The Ames Straw Poll died a quiet death in the summer of 2011, although the patient didn't realize it was all over until five months later.

For the better part of three decades, the straw poll, held on the campus of Iowa State University, amounted to a must-attend event. Though it was nothing more than a fund-raiser for the Iowa Republican Party, it transformed itself—with a major assist from the mainstream media (shakes fist)—into an early indicator of who might wind up winning the first-in-the-nation caucuses in the Hawkeye State.

In 1979, 1987, and 1999 the straw poll winner went on to win the caucuses. In 2007, former Arkansas governor Mike Huckabee—remember him?—came in a surprising second at Ames and went on to win in Iowa the following year.

As the supposed importance of Ames as organizational litmus test grew, so too did the pageantry surrounding it. By the time George W.

Bush and Steve Forbes faced off in 1999, it had become a full-blown carnival.

In a parking lot outside of the Hilton Coliseum—where Cyclone hoops greats like Fred "The Mayor" Hoiberg and Marcus "Huge NBA Bust" Fizer (OK, that wasn't his nickname) once roamed, the Iowa GOP auctioned off the various parcels around the voting site to the aspirants. In 1999, Bush, who was practically bathing in cash, dropped $40,000 just to have the best and biggest space in the Coliseum parking lot. In 2011, Texas representative Ron Paul was the highest bidder—spending $31,000 for his plot.

Once their piece of land—concrete, actually—was secured, the real spending began. Elaborate tents and stages were built, caterers were hired to feed the masses, dunking booths were set up, tickets were bought for attendees. (Yes, one of the great/terrible things about Ames is that the candidates paid for their "supporters" to attend.)

And the media swarmed. And I do mean swarmed. More than eight hundred press credentials were issued for the 2011 version of Ames, which amounted to more votes than either former Massachusetts governor Mitt Romney or former House Speaker Newt Gingrich received at the event itself. Reporters from Japan, Germany, and every American news outlet you have ever heard of—and many you haven't heard of—circled those few days in mid-August as a must-do for campaign coverage.

With reporters literally everywhere, political hangers-on were drawn to Ames like flies to a carcass. (And, yes, I am aware I just compared the media—of which I am a member—to an insect that vomits its own food.) National Rifle Association supporters paraded around Ames wearing orange hats. Men dressed like Uncle Sam and women dressed like Lady Liberty were a dime a dozen. And everywhere, everywhere were people pushing pet causes that ranged from the mildly credible to the demonstrably insane.

Over the years, reporters covering Ames grew ever more cynical about the event—and what it told us about the Republican race. After all, no more than 23,000 people had *ever* voted at Ames—in 2007 just 14,000 did—and the idea of it as a must-stop for political candidates was fading rapidly. But cover it they did—and did, and did, and did.

The 2011 Ames straw poll changed all that. First, Romney, who had been the favorite since it became clear he was running for president again (and that became clear about five minutes after he dropped out of the 2008 race), bowed out—insisting that any straw polls were a waste of time and energy for his campaign.

But Romney isn't the one who, ultimately, stuck the dagger in the heart of Ames. That honor goes to Minnesota representative Michele Bachmann.

And it's beyond ironic—in that Alanis Morissette way—that it was Bachmann who killed the straw poll. After all, Bachmann rode to prominence in Iowa by touting the fact that she was born in Waterloo and, therefore, understood the hopes, dreams, and problems of the state's residents better than the outsiders trying to home in on their votes.

It worked—for a while. Bachmann surged over the summer months, and when straw poll day—August 13, 2011—came it was clear that she was the favorite. Her tent was the largest of any on the grounds, and there was a steady stream of people angling to get inside for the chance to glimpse the candidate herself. (Oddly, once you made it inside the tent, which had all its flaps down to keep in the air-conditioning, it wasn't all-so-spectacular. Between the cool temperatures and the darkness it reminded me more of a cave than anything else.)

No one was surprised then when the straw poll results were announced and Bachmann had won—albeit very narrowly over Paul. (Much more about Paul—and the cultlike following he has developed—later.)

What few people realized at the time was that Ames marked not the beginning of the beginning of Bachmann's run as a top-tier candidate but instead the beginning of the end. Even as the straw poll results were being read, Texas governor Rick Perry was announcing his decision to enter the race—and it only got worse from there for Bachmann.

The following day, at a Lincoln Day Dinner in Blackhawk County—yes, that is really the name of the county—Bachmann and Perry were both scheduled to speak. The Bachmann forces saw it as a chance to engage Perry on their terms—after all, they were just coming off of a huge straw poll victory, and the Texas governor was just now entering the race. Instead it turned into a symbol of everything that was to go wrong for Bachmann as summer turned to fall.

While Perry worked the room, displaying the sort of natural charm that voters saw too little of in the campaign, Bachmann's famous/infamous campaign bus was circling the venue. The candidate refused to enter the dinner until Perry had cleared out. When she did, finally, speak, she was "horrible," according to a former adviser to the candidate. The practical effect of her circling the target was that Perry had already won the room and the media coverage of the event. RICK PERRY SCHOOLS MICHELE BACHMANN IN WATERLOO read the headline from a Politico story on the event.

Things went from bad to worse for Bachmann. Perry having stolen her thunder, Bachmann watched her support erode badly—both in Iowa and nationally. She kept up a brave face. Try to find a picture from those months where she isn't smiling. Seriously. We dare you. And to her credit, she did well in her increasingly limited role in the dozen (or so) debates during the fall.

By the time Iowans voted—a whole three days into 2012!—Bachmann's political obituary and that of the Ames straw poll had already been written. Bachmann won 4,823 votes in the Ames straw poll. One hundred forty-four days later, she got just 6,046 votes in the actual Iowa caucuses—good (that may not be the right word) for sixth place. It's actually even worse than it sounds. Only six candidates were actively competing in Iowa; former Utah governor Jon Huntsman skipped the state entirely but managed 739 votes. (Rick Santorum, the former Pennsylvania senator who won the Iowa caucuses, finished fourth at the straw poll with 9 percent.)

Bachmann's first-to-worst performance ends the Ames straw poll as a barometer of much of anything in Iowa Republican politics. Yes, it will continue. And, yes, defenders of the straw poll will insist the Bachmann victory/collapse was the exception, not the rule. And, triple yes, the media will almost certainly continue to cover it as though it means something.

But smart politicos—and I am nominating myself for this category—now should know better. Ames was always, at root, a fund-raiser masked as an actual contest; after all, in what other election do you buy people tickets to attend and vote for you? Bachmann's victory laid bare the utter meaninglessness of the Ames straw poll as a predictive or productive exercise.

Ames died that day in mid-August 2011 at the hands of one of its own—Michele Bachmann. Let's hope it stays dead.

And in its place? (The Fix is all about solutions, after all.) How about an *American Idol*–like competition in which each week the candidates are tested on various skills they'll need to make it in the presidential race.

Think about it. One week they could do the "major aspirational/inspirational speech." Another week it could be working a rope line. Or dealing with the fallout from a scandal in your campaign. Or kissing babies. Or dealing with a hostile audience. How about a mock debate? I mean, the possibilities are literally endless.

At the end of every week, America would vote on who did it the best. I mean, this is a democracy after all. The lowest vote-getter would get a chance to argue for his political life in front of a three-person panel of judges—me, Katie Couric, and Bill Clinton (like he wouldn't totally want to participate)—and then would have judgment rendered. You get kicked off, you drop out. And so it goes until we get down to a final four candidates, at which point we begin the traditional nominating contest.

Is there *any* question that the level of interest in politics would shoot through the roof? With the public voting every week there would be a genuine engagement well beyond what we currently see in the early days of a primary race. It would also take money out of the process—at least at the start. Rather than spending the lion's share of their time trolling for cash, the candidates would dedicate themselves to perfecting skills they actually would need if/when they managed to be elected president.

Plus, is allowing the public to choose their final four candidates via a *Political Idol* competition any more arbitrary than the way we currently do it? No way.

# THE BEST POLITICAL BLOGROLL— ANYWHERE

People always ask me what I read on a daily basis. Answer: not all that much. I skim. So, then, what do I skim? That's easier. Below is the most comprehensive blogroll I—plus some of my smarty-pants friends—could think of. Rip these pages out of the book and put them next to (or in) your computer. You'll need them this fall.

### FROM THE RIGHT

Jim Geraghty, Campaign Spot: http://www.nationalreview.com/campaign-spot

Hot Air: http://hotair.com/

American Spectator blog: http://spectator.org/blog

Michael Dougherty: http://www.businessinsider.com/author/michael-brendan-dougherty

## DOWN THE MIDDLE
Nate Silver: http://fivethirtyeight.blogs.nytimes.com/
Christian Heinze: http://gop12.thehill.com/

## FROM THE LEFT
Steve Benen: http://maddowblog.msnbc.msn.com/
Jonathan Bernstein, Plain Blog: http://plainblogaboutpolitics
    .blogspot.com/
The Monkey Cage: http://themonkeycage.org/
ThinkProgress: http://thinkprogress.org/
Ezra Klein, Wonkblog: http://www.washingtonpost.com/blogs/
    ezra-klein
Greg Sargent, The Plum Line: http://www.washingtonpost
    .com/blogs/plum-line

# THE BEST STATE POLITICAL BLOGROLL— ANYWHERE

National blogs may get all the attention (present company included), but for the true political junkie (present company included), there's a whole other level of terrific blogging going on at the state level.

We've collected our favorite(s) from each of the fifty states. Bookmark them. There's no better way to follow Senate, governor, and House races than through these state-specific blogs.

### ALABAMA
*Doc's Political Parlor*
*Left in Alabama*
*Wanted Alabama Democrats*

### ALASKA
*The Mudflats*

## ARIZONA
*Arizona Eagletarian*
*Espresso Pundit*

## ARKANSAS
*Arkansas Blog*
*Tolbert Report*

## CALIFORNIA
*Calbuzz*
*California Majority Report*
*California's Capitol*
*Capitol Alert*
*Carla Marinucci*
*Fox and Hounds Daily*
*Rough & Tumble*

## COLORADO
*Colorado Peak Politics*
*Colorado Pols*
*Complete Colorado*
*Peoples Press Collective*
*The Spot*
*Square State*

## CONNECTICUT
*CT Capitol Report*
*My Left Nutmeg*

## DELAWARE
*Delaware Grapevine*
*Delaware Liberal*

## FLORIDA
*Sayfie Review*
*Bizpacreview*
*The Buzz*
*Florida Progressive Coalition*
*Naked Politics*
*Political Pulse*
*SaintPetersBlog*
*The Spencerian*
*Sunshine State News*

## GEORGIA
*Peach Pundit*
*Political Insider*

## HAWAII
*All Hawaii News*

## IDAHO
*43rd State Blues*
*Huckleberries Online*
*Idaho Reporter*

## ILLINOIS
*Capitol Fax*
*Chicago Current*
*Illinois Review*

## INDIANA
*Capitol & Washington*
*Hoosier Access*
*Indiana Barrister*

## IOWA
*The Bean Walker*
*Bleeding Heartland*
*Iowa Independent*
*Iowa Republican*
*John Deeth*
*Under the Golden Dome*

## KANSAS
*Dome on the Range*
*Hawver's News*

## KENTUCKY
*Barefoot and Progressive*
*Bluegrass Bulletin*
*Hillbilly Report*
*Page One Kentucky*

## LOUISIANA
*Between the Lines*
*Daily Kingfish*
*The Hayride*

## MAINE
*Dirigo Blue*
*Maine Politics*
*Pine Tree Politics*

## MARYLAND
*Maryland Reporter*
*Red Maryland*

## MASSACHUSETTS
*Blue Mass Group*
*Political Intelligence*
*Talking Politics*

## MICHIGAN
*Blogging for Michigan*
*Jack Lessenberry*
*Right Michigan*

## MINNESOTA
*Bluestem Prairie*
*Capitol View*
*Dump Bachmann*
*Hot Dish Politics*
*Minnesota Independent*
*MinnPotus*
*MN Progressive Project*
*Smart Politics*
*True North*

## MISSISSIPPI
*Cotton Mouth Blog*
*Majority in Mississippi*
*Y'all Politics*

## MISSOURI
*Fired Up! Missouri*
*Politicmo*
*Show Me Progress*

## MONTANA
*Intelligent Discontent*
*Montana Cowgirl*

## NEBRASKA
*Leavenworth Street*
*New Nebraska*
*Winterized*

## NEVADA
*Desert Beacon*
*In the Sausage Factory*
*Inside Nevada Politics*
*Las Vegas Gleaner*
*The Nevada View*
*Nevada News Bureau*
*Slash Politics*
*Ralston Flash*

## NEW HAMPSHIRE
*Blue Hampshire*
*NH Journal*
*WMUR Political Scoop*

## NEW JERSEY
*Blue Jersey*
*PolitickerNJ*
*Save Jersey*

## NEW MEXICO
*Democracy for New Mexico*

*Heath Haussamen*
*Joe Monahan*

## NEW YORK
*The Albany Project*
*Capitol Confidential*
*The Daily Politics*
*State of Politics*

## NORTH CAROLINA
*Cape Fear Watchdogs*
*Capital Beat*
*Civitas Review*
*NCCapitol*
*Talking About Politics*
*Under the Dome*

## NORTH DAKOTA
*Flickertales from the Hill*
*North Decoder*
*Say Anything*

## OHIO
*Plunderbund*
*Ohio Daily Blog*
*The Sidney Independent*
*Third Base Politics*

## OKLAHOMA
*BatesLine*
*The McCarville Report*
*Muskogee Politico*

## OREGON
*Blue Oregon*
*Capitol Watch*
*Jeff Mapes*
*Oregon Catalyst*

## PENNSYLVANIA
*Politics PA*
*Capitol Ideas*
*Early Returns*
*2 Political Junkies*

## RHODE ISLAND
*On Politics/WRNI*
*Nesi's Notes*

## SOUTH CAROLINA
*FITS News*
*Political Briefing*

## SOUTH DAKOTA
*Madville Times*
*South Dakota War College*

## TENNESSEE
*Camp4U*
*Humphrey on the Hill*
*Knox Views*
*PostPolitics*

## TEXAS
*Texas Tribune*
*Burka Blog*
*Burnt Orange Report*

## UTAH
*Out of Context*
*Utah Policy*

## VERMONT
*Green Mountain Daily*
*Vermont Daily Briefing*
*VTdigger*

## VIRGINIA
*Bearing Drift*
*Blue Virginia*
*Not Larry Sabato*

## WASHINGTON
*NPI Advocate*
*NW Daily Marker*
*Petri Dish*
*Political Buzz*
*Politics Northwest*
*Slog*
*Strange Bedfellows*

## WEST VIRGINIA
*West Virginia Blue*

## WISCONSIN
*Blogging Blue*
*Blue Cheddar*
*Dane 101*
*On Politics*
*Uppity Wisconsin*
*WisPolitics*

## WYOMING
*Hummingbirdminds*
*The Pitch*
*Wyoming Capitol Journal*

# THE NOT TOP TEN— THE TEN ISSUES YOU WON'T HEAR ABOUT THIS FALL

"It's the economy, stupid."

Truer political words were never spoken. James Carville and George Stephanopoulos made that phrase famous during Bill Clinton's 1992 run for president, but it matters as much today as it did twenty years ago.

The economy is the only issue on voters' minds. More than six in ten Floridians, South Carolinians, and New Hampshirites told exit pollsters that the economy was the most important issue to them. Every national poll conducted over the past three years has shown something very similar.

You would have to be a real dummy—and given that you have bought this book you obviously are not—to miss that the 2012 election will be decided by the state of the economy.

The politics of the economy are fascinating to behold. All of politics is a struggle between reality and perception, and no place is that yin/yang more apparent than when it comes to how voters feel about the economy. The perception that things are getting better leads people to create an economic reality to fit that optimism; they buy a car, or a house, or a mobile home—best of both worlds!—which in turn makes the economy grow. All you need to do is look at the last three years to know that the inverse is also true. If people feel bad about where the country's fiscal future is headed, they hold on to their money—Scrooge McDuck style. But we digress . . .

If the economy is sucking up every ounce of oxygen in the political room—bad (and extended!) metaphor alert—then what other issues are being suffocated? What would we—and the candidates—be talking about if they weren't talking about the economy all the damn time?

In honor of *SportsCenter*—aka the show that Mrs. Fix demands be turned off when I am watching it straight through for the second consecutive hour—we give you the Not Top Ten Issues of 2012.

## 1. IMMIGRATION

There are eleven million people here illegally. Everyone knows that the option pushed by most Republicans—round them all up and send them home—is both logistically impossible and, perhaps more importantly, ridiculously expensive. Mitt Romney's suggestion in a January debate that the solution was self-deportation, which is exactly what it sounds like, is equally laughable. "OK, if you are here illegally, please step forward. Thanks. Terrific."

Hispanics, who make up the fastest-growing minority community in the country, are, not surprisingly, somewhat put off by the Republicans' "get 'em all out, *now*" approach to the issue. In the 2008 election, Barack Obama beat John McCain, a senator from a border state who had made a genuine effort to lead his party toward the middle on immigration, 67 percent to 33 percent.

That sparked an "uh-oh" moment for smart Republicans across the country, who readily admit that if they allow Hispanics to become a reliably Democratic constituency for the foreseeable future, their future as a majority party is, in a word, over. You, of course, wouldn't know it by watching the Republican primary race earlier this year where the candidates—with the somewhat odd exceptions of Newt Gingrich and Rick Perry—fell all over themselves to run to the (far) right on the issue.

So heated did the rhetoric grow over immigration that Jeb Bush, the paterfamilias of sorts within the modern-day GOP, called for caution—warning that the candidates' "tone" could cost them in swing states this November. A sampling of those swing states proves Bush's point: New Mexico (46 percent Hispanic by population), Arizona (29.6 percent), Nevada (26.5 percent), Florida (22.5 percent), and Colorado (20.7 percent). Add up just those five states and you get fifty-nine electoral votes, more than one-quarter of the total a presidential candidate needs to win in November.

The math is bad news for Republicans. But Democrats won't/don't talk much about immigration either. Why? Because they need white voters—particularly in states like Arizona, Florida, and Colorado—to go their way in the fall, and they know that many whites hate the idea of granting citizenship to any—*any*—person here illegally. Need proof? In Barack Obama's 2012 State of the Union address, which totaled more than 6,000 words, a total of 195 were dedicated—in whole or part—to the issue of immigration. Overlooked? Yes. Unbelievably important to the future of both parties? Yes.

## 2. HEALTH CARE

The signal achievement—in terms of major policy accomplishments—of President Obama's first term in office was passage of the Affordable Care Act, a broad overhaul of the way in which health care is delivered in this country. And yet, in his 2012 State of the Union address, President Obama mentioned health care a total of 0 times. Yes, *zero*. As in none. Nada. Zilch. Zippy.

That silence is a sign that Obama and his senior strategy team have given up on winning politically on health care, a major shift from the days after the bill's passage in March 2010, when they pledged that the law would be a net positive for the president as he sought a second term.

What the White House underestimated was how badly they had lost the message war over health care to Republicans. A look at monthly tracking polls sponsored by the Kaiser Family Foundation tells the story of the law. For the better part of the last eighteen months, public opinion has barely moved—with roughly 40 percent of people supportive of the law and 44 percent (or so) disapproving. Nothing—not word that the Supreme Court would rule on the constitutionality of the individual mandate, not implementation of a variety of seemingly popular provisions—impacts those numbers in any statistically significant way. Public opinion is absolutely set as it relates to the health care law, and set in such a way that it does little good for President Obama to trumpet it on the campaign trail.

Expect him to mention the bill in front of Democratic audiences occasionally as he seeks to prove that he did the hard things that progressives wanted despite significant Republican opposition. Independent and swing voters are far less receptive to that message, however, and that's who Obama needs to win over heading into November. And so, mum will be the word on health care.

## 3. EDUCATION

To listen to President Obama's 2012 State of the Union speech, you might think that education reform was going to be a major focus for him in the year leading up to the November election. He mentioned education on thirteen separate occasions in the address and rolled out a series of proposals, including a call for states to mandate that kids stay in high school until they graduate or, at a minimum, turn eighteen.

That makes for a nice line in a speech, but you won't find a single political person who believes there will be any real movement on education reforms between now and November. The last major overhaul of the education system—the No Child Left Behind Act—came more than a decade ago and, despite passing both chambers of Congress with overwhelming support, has now become mired in a largely partisan debate over the efficacy of its means testing and the broader philosophical questions of how involved the federal government should be in education.

Talking about education in politics is smart because no matter a voter's party affiliation, he/she is generally in favor of spending more money on educating our kids. But in this economic climate, spending any more federal money is simply a nonstarter for either Obama or Romney.

## 4. DEBT REDUCTION

There's no doubt there will be plenty of talk about the need to reduce the country's debt—$15 trillion and growing—but little in the way of specifics about how that could actually happen.

If the way Congress "resolved" the debt ceiling fight in the summer of 2011 is any indication, we won't hear much of anything in the way of solutions on debt matters. After spending months and months debating whether to raise the borrowing limit on the nation's credit card, Congress pulled a classic kick-the-can-down-the-road move by creating a so-called super committee that would make the tough cuts to begin reducing the deficit by the end of 2011. Or not. With the super committee members appointed by the Democratic and Republican leadership in the House and Senate, the panel was doomed from the start. (Why would any party leader appoint people to a super committee who they had reason to believe might cut a deal with the other side that could have major long-term political implications? It was just never going to happen.)

Elections are, at least on the policy front, telling people what they want to hear—"No new taxes," "It's morning in America," etc.—not speaking hard truths about the perilous economic position our government has put us in. Running on a "we are going to need to raise taxes *and* cut services" platform has about the same chance of success as me beating LeBron James in a game of one-on-one. That's why Obama and Romney will talk around the debt rather than about it.

## 5. ENERGY

The public focuses on the future of American energy when gas prices go up. But as soon as prices regulate to whatever the new normal is, the issue disappears from view.

Though very few politicians are talking about it, there's actually good news on the energy front; domestic oil output is the highest it has been since the early 2000s, and the country is producing natural gas like gangbusters. Those developments have led to a reversal of America's seemingly ever-growing dependence on foreign sources to meet our energy needs; roughly 81 percent of those needs were met by domestic sources through the first ten months of 2011, according to a survey conducted by Bloomberg News.

Still, the wild fluctuations in gas prices—a gallon of gas costs you more than $4 in some parts of the country this spring—speaks to how depending on crude oil from a region as unstable as the Middle East is a shaky policy going forward.

President Obama is doing all he can to link energy policy to economic policy, announcing in his 2012 State of the Union address his plan to expand natural gas drilling from shale deposits—an effort he says will create as many as 600,000 jobs. But the American public has yet to really make the link between energy and the economy in their own collective mind, ensuring that this is a back-burner—see what we did there?—issue in November.

## 6 AND 7. FOREIGN POLICY (IT'S SO IMPORTANT AND SO IGNORED THAT IT GETS TWO SPOTS!)

At a time when the United States remains committed—at varying levels—to ongoing conflicts in Iraq and Afghanistan, when the prospect of a nuclear Iran seems more real than ever before, and when the rise of China threatens our supremacy as the lone world superpower, the American public offers a collective shoulder shrug when it comes to foreign policy.

Take the state of South Carolina, for example. Its large military population should make it a place where the discussion of how and when our troops should be used in foreign lands would be particularly relevant. And yet, when the Republican presidential primary swept through the state in mid-January, no foreign policy issue even made it into the top four voter concerns. (Sixty-three percent of people said the economy was the most important issue facing the country, while another 22 percent named the budget deficit.)

Or the candidacy of former Utah governor Jon Huntsman, who returned from a stint as the U.S. ambassador to China to run for president in 2012. Huntsman premised his candidacy on his unique ability to understand America's role in the world because he had—in his own words—seen our country from "10,000 miles" away. The Republican electorate didn't care at all, focusing far more on Huntsman's work for the Obama administration and his moderate tone on the stump. His campaign failed to launch in New Hampshire and he dropped out of the race soon afterward, endorsing Romney.

(I still remember well a trip I took to give a handful of speeches in Europe after the 2008 election. The first question always asked of me was what the average American voter thought of Europe. Overcoming worries about offending my hosts, I would tell them bluntly, "The average American doesn't think of Europe. At all." Sad but true.)

The simple reality of American politics is that even in the best of economic times at home, most voters don't know or care about foreign policy. That goes double—or more—when economic times are, as they are now, tough. With people worried about making their mortgage payments, affording their kids' education, and making tomorrow better than today, what is happening in Syria, the Middle East, or just about anywhere else doesn't matter a whit to people.

To the extent foreign policy will play any role at all in the fall election, it will be in terms of a discussion of when American troops need to come home from Afghanistan. Polling conducted in the spring of 2012 suggests that as many as seven in ten Americans oppose the war in Afghanistan, while majorities said we should bring our troops home regardless of whether the Afghanis can protect themselves. Even so, barring some huge flare-up in the country, that feels like a subsidiary issue—at most.

The truth of the matter is that the challenges posed by Iran, the Middle East, and various other hot spots around the world could well be front-burner issues for whoever wins the White House this fall. But you won't know it by watching the two men campaign for that job.

## 8. CAMPAIGN FINANCE

Ask anyone with even a passing interest in politics about whether there is too much money flowing through the system and you'll almost certainly be greeted with a resounding "Yes!" After all, one of the biggest stories of the 2012 election is and will continue to be the spending of super PACS, new fund-raising vehicles that allow a single wealthy individual—or a posse of wealthy individuals—to fund ads bringing down or lifting up a candidate.

But, for all the foul-crying regarding the amount of cashola washing around the political system, the simple fact is that, while the average person may say they care about changing the way campaigns are financed, they simply don't vote on the issue.

Go back to the 2000 Senate campaign between former Goldman Sachs executive Jon Corzine and Representative Bob Franks. Corzine spent upwards of $60 million of his own money on the race, while Franks, not gifted with extraordinary wealth, raised and spent about $6 million. In an attempt to level the playing field, Franks focused the entirety of his campaign on the idea that Corzine was trying to buy a Senate seat and was using his personal money to cover up his thin political résumé. Franks's problem? Corzine's money bought him lots—and lots—of TV ads across the state of New Jersey, ads that drowned out the message Franks was trying to send. Corzine won—and went on to be elected governor of New Jersey five years later by spending another $43 million of his own cash. (Money doesn't buy you love, though. Corzine was ousted in his 2009 reelection race by Chris Christie.)

There are myriad other examples of this phenomenon. President Obama breaking his promise to accept public financing in the 2008 general election because he knew he could raise drastically more money on his own is one. And all of them point to an undeniable political fact: voters say they care about campaign finance reform, but virtually no one votes on it. Given that, politicians tend not to talk about it unless prompted—and that is very likely to be the case as the campaign for president wears on.

Both President Obama and Mitt Romney will decry the influence of outside groups in the 2012 election, but neither will do anything meaningful to prevent money from being spent by these groups to savage their opponent because they know there will be little (or no) price to pay from voters.

## 9. GUN CONTROL

The attempted assassination of former Arizona congresswoman Gabrielle Giffords in January 2011 shocked the nation and the world. Giffords had been in the process of holding an event in her Tucson-area district when a deranged gunman approached her, shot her in the head, and went on to murder six other people, including a nine-year-old girl, a federal judge, and Giffords's director of community outreach. President Obama traveled to Arizona for a memorial service to honor Giffords and the victims and delivered one of the best—and most moving—speeches of his presidency. In that address he declared: "Already we've seen a national conversation commence, not only about the motivations behind these killings, but about everything from the merits of gun safety laws to the adequacy of our mental health systems."

And yet, no major changes in gun control laws were made. It's a familiar pattern. In the wake of mass shootings—Columbine and Virginia Tech jump to mind—there is a hue and cry from some circles that the country must do a better job at regulating who can buy guns. Some measures are proposed and approved, but they tend to be things that nibble at the margins of gun control rather than genuinely change the game on gun ownership. Why? That's a harder question to answer.

There's been very little polling done on gun issues in recent years—a testament to how far it's fallen off the political radar—but what is out there suggests that people generally favor more strict guns laws. A *Time* magazine poll in June 2011 showed 51 percent of people favored stricter gun laws, while 39 percent said gun laws in the country should be left alone and 7 percent said they should be made less strict.

The reluctance among politicians to push for more strictures on your right to bear arms then isn't born of public disdain for the idea. Rather, it has to do with the power of the gun lobby and the concern many Democrats have that pushing for strong gun laws allows Republicans to paint them as out-of-touch urbanites with little understanding of the middle of the country.

On the first point, the National Rifle Association (NRA) is among the best-organized lobbying groups in Washington. The NRA keeps a close eye on attempts to impinge on gun rights anywhere in the country and is not afraid to use its lobbying might to make very clear to wavering politicians the dangers of crossing it.

On the second, Democrats have, over the past decade, walked back much of their gun control rhetoric as they have worked to remake the party's image among rural voters in swing states. Fearful of being tagged with the "liberal" label, Democratic politicians— particularly in the South and Midwest—have walked away from talking about gun control in anything but the broadest of terms. Democrats are also mindful of the losses they incurred in the 1994 election, defeats blamed, at least in part, on the passage of the Assault Weapons Ban, which then president Bill Clinton had pushed through Congress earlier that year. (It is not by accident that when the Assault Weapons Ban came up for re-authorization in 2004, Congress did not give it.)

President Obama promised action on guns in the wake of the Giffords shooting. No such action has come. And moving on gun control between now and November would amount to a kamikaze mission—not something successful politicians are in the habit of embarking on.

## 10. TERRORISM

America is now eleven years removed from the attacks of September 11, 2001. While anxiety still lingers within the body politic about the possibility of another attack in the United States, the political potency of the issue seems to have faded.

Both President Obama and Mitt Romney will talk about the importance of keeping Americans safe from the threat of terrorism. And Obama will almost certainly use his authorization of a mission that killed Osama bin Laden to bolster his national security credentials.

But in an odd way, the death of bin Laden—not to mention the killings of a variety of other top al Qaeda lieutenants in the last few years—has made the issue of terrorism feel less relevant, less real to the average person. With the face of terrorism for most Americans now dead, it's no longer the sort of top-of-mind issue it was even in the 2008 campaign, although, even in that race, the political power of terrorism had already begun to fade somewhat. Former New York City mayor Rudy Giuliani premised the entirety of his presidential bid in 2008 on the role he played during the attacks. Voters weren't moved; Giuliani didn't win a single state before dropping from the contest.

Terrorism hovers—and likely always will hover—like a dark cloud on the horizon of most Americans' consciousness. But that dark cloud is far away at the moment, so far off it seems to be almost totally out of sight.

# PURITAN BACKROOM:

## Chicken Fingers and the New Hampshire Primary

Manchester, New Hampshire, is not exactly a culinary hot spot. Eating three meals in a single day at Dunkin' Donuts is not (entirely) unheard of. Restaurants in the Queen City—not kidding, that is Manchester's nickname—tend to close on the early side too, which makes for slim pickings for a hungry campaign reporter returning to home base after a day of driving the Granite State.

Enter the Puritan Backroom, the best little restaurant—and political must-stop—in the state. Where else can you in the back eat a heaping of the best chicken fingers this side of, well, anywhere and then stroll/roll around to the front for some ice cream, all the while carrying a fifty-fifty chance of seeing a presidential candidate doing the exact same thing?

The Puritan's successful run in New Hampshire goes back well before the state moved its primary to the front of the presidential nominating calendar in 1976. It was founded in 1917 as an ice cream and candy shop, but a year later a restaurant was added. The original

Puritan location was across the street from city hall in downtown Manchester. "Right from the beginning politics was regularly infused into the business," said Chris Pappas, the current owner of the business. (His great-grandfather—Arthur Pappas—was one of the restaurant's original founders.)

Though the Puritan has now moved just outside of downtown Manchester, it has established itself as a must-stop for politicians trying to reach the ever-flinty (and somewhat indecisive) New Hampshire primary voter.

Sargent Shriver loved the Puritan so much that he ended virtually every day he spent in the state during the 1972 presidential race with a dinner of barbecued lamb kabobs at the restaurant. Joe Lieberman was at the Puritan so much during his 2004 presidential bid that the restaurant not only named a flavor of ice cream after him ("Cup of Joe") but also did the same for his wife, Hadassah ("Heavenly Hadassah")! Bob Kerrey, the former Nebraska senator, tended bar for a night at the Puritan in support of Al Gore's 2000 New Hampshire campaign. New Mexico governor Bill Richardson held his 2008 primary night "party" at the Puritan. (He finished fourth with 4.6 percent of the vote.)

In the final weekend before that 2008 New Hampshire primary, Hillary Clinton rented out the Puritan's conference center and turned it into a call center; she even held a get-out-the-vote rally in the Puritan parking lot forty-eight hours before her comeback victory in the Granite State. "I like to think all the chicken tenders and coffee for the volunteers fueled her upset victory," said Pappas. (Worth noting: Barack Obama is one of the few presidential aspirants to have never set foot in the Puritan. Draw your own conclusions.)

On the Saturday before the Tuesday primary in 2012, former Utah governor Jon Huntsman and his wife stopped by the Puritan to pick up an order of bulk chicken tenders—yum—as a thank-you for his staff and supporters. "The place was basically shut down for the ten minutes he was here and we had to usher him out through the kitchen because the crush of media was so huge," said Pappas. (He noted that a few months earlier Huntsman had stopped by the Puritan with only a few staff in tow to shake hands; the full-court crush of media and other political hangers-on begins about two months before the actual vote.) The Puritan magic did not work for Huntsman; he finished third.

Heck, even Sarah Palin, that most famous of (non)candidates, stopped by the Puritan the night before a Tea Party rally at the statehouse in September 2011. Like most of Palin's political events, this one was unannounced and "caused a stir," recounted Pappas. A couple was getting married at the restaurant that night and posed for pictures with Palin. "We'll never forget that Sarah Palin came to our wedding," the couple was overheard saying. I'll bet.

Pappas says the restaurant's centrality to the New Hampshire political landscape is due in large part to the cross section of Granite Staters it attracts. He explained: "We have our share of elderly customers who have been coming here for decades. We draw business types for lunch and families for dinner and on the weekends. Younger people come out for the chicken tenders and mudslides."

About those tenders, of which I have consumed dozens during my trips to New Hampshire: the Puritan started making them in the mid-1970s as a favor to their chicken supplier, who had pieces left over after cutting up chicken breasts for the menu. Pappas said that the tenders "took off immediately," and the restaurant now sells more than 1,000 pounds of tenders a day. (That's a *lot* of tenders.) How are they so much better than your run-of-the-mill grossness from McDonald's and Burger King? "They're marinated overnight, breaded and fried to order, and served with homemade sweet-and-sour sauce," explains Pappas. "They're different from many others because the chicken is real chicken meat (not processed), and the marinade gives them a unique sweet flavor."

The Puritan—and its rich political history and chicken tenders—speaks to the centrality of retail politicking to running a presidential primary campaign.

Even in this age of twenty-four-hour cable news, Twitter, and people texting their friends who happen to be sitting right next to them, places like the Puritan prove that there is still no replacement for gripping and grinning with voters.

The first three states in both the Republican and Democratic presidential nomination fights—Iowa, New Hampshire, and South Carolina—are all states in which retail politics is still king (or queen).

When Rudy Giuliani, the former mayor of New York City, made his maiden visit to Iowa during his 2008 presidential campaign, he traveled in a phalanx of black SUVs—speeding from stop to stop with virtually no unscripted interaction with actual voters. Not even the man who was credited with leading the country through the terrorist attacks of September 11, 2001, could get away with acting like that. Iowa voters balked. As did New Hampshire voters. And South Carolina voters. Giuliani staked his campaign on the decidedly non-retail state of Florida—the way to win in the Sunshine State is to just dump millions of dollars on television—but by the time the race got to that point, it was already over for Giuliani.

The man who surged in his place? Mike Huckabee, the former governor of Arkansas, whom no one had heard of until he started showing up at every meeting where two or more Iowans were gathered. Huckabee got retail politicking in a way no one else in the field—not John McCain and certainly not Mitt Romney—did. Huckabee loved the hurly-burly of politics in a way not seen since the last politician from Hope, Arkansas—a guy named William Jefferson Clinton—hit the national stage.

The ability to actually talk to other human beings is underrated in our political process. After all, if you can't relate in ways small and big to the people you want to represent, why should you be representing them at all?

Campaigns aren't won on paper. If they were, Bill Bradley (Rhodes scholar, NBA great, U.S. senator) would be president and Meg Whitman (billionaire executive) would be the governor of California. Places like the Puritan and the Iowa State Fair and any number of barbecue joints in South Carolina force candidates to prove their mettle, to wade into a group of skeptics and convince them.

For those who argue that retail politics has little to do with what you actually do when you are elected president, here's my response: What is diplomacy if not using your powers of persuasion to convince foreign leaders of the rightness of a certain course of action? And how do you get your signature pieces of legislation through Congress? Convincing a relatively small group of influential leaders that you understand their concerns and believe this is the right course for them to take.

Retail politics is at the heart of who we are—or at least who we should be—as a body politic. The Puritan Backroom isn't just about stuffing your face full of chicken tenders—although that's not a bad option. It's about showing and proving you have what it takes to represent the hopes and dreams of an entire country.

# WHAT IT TAKES TO WRITE *WHAT IT TAKES*

It takes more than two hours to get to Richard Ben Cramer's house from Washington, DC. You have to cross a major body of water—the Chesapeake Bay—and navigate a series of increasingly narrow two-lane roads to make it there. His driveway isn't paved. You get the idea.

"Washington is a very corrosive town," Ben Cramer says as he lights—and then relights—cigar after cigar. The ashtray on his desk is filled with their stub-ends. The desk sits in a sparsely furnished shack that functions as Ben Cramer's writing room. The shack sits on the back end of a large plot of land dominated by an old white farmhouse where Ben Cramer and his wife—they were married on Valentine's Day 2012 in Philadelphia—live. It's in a quiet nook of the

Eastern Shore of Maryland not far from where Ben Cramer wrote *What It Takes,* a 1,000-page recounting of the 1988 presidential race that focused not on what the candidates said on the campaign trail but on who they were before they became who they are. *What It Takes* was a reimagining of how to cover campaigns—a process that up to that point had been defined by the straight narrative retellings offered by the likes of Teddy White (*The Making of the President* series) and Jack Germond and Jules Witcover.

"They didn't answer what I wanted to know," Ben Cramer said of those journalists. What was that? "I couldn't figure out why these [politicians] who must have been big guys . . . why did they look like such little putzes on TV screens—saying stuff that no human being would say to his wife or family or friends. That's what I wanted to do."

> His was a solitary battle, maddeningly slow. The nurses could lift him out of traction, help him off his bed, but after that, it was up to Bob how many baby steps he could take. One day, by act of will, he might walk to the end of the hall, and his hope for a miracle would swell again. He was going to make it back, whole, good as new—back at school, he'd play for Phog Allen. . . . But then, the next morning, in the whirlpool, a therapist might work for two hours, unsuccessfully, trying to gently pry two fingers apart on the claw of his right hand. Or Dole might lie in traction all day, trying, until sweat rolled down his face, to move two fingers together, on his left hand. And if he could not, the world went black, and there was Dole alone again, just his will—that was all he recognized of himself—trapped in a hospital bed with his nemesis, this body.
>
> —Richard Ben Cramer on Bob Dole

Before I go into exactly what it was that Ben Cramer did with *What It Takes,* a digression is in order. I first met Ben Cramer in 2010 when he got word—through a kid named Jack Bohrer, who was a helpmate to him and is now a speechwriter for Maryland governor Martin O'Malley—that a group of young journalists believed that his 1988 campaign chronicle was the ur-text of political reporting done right.

Along with Politico's Jonathan Martin, BuzzFeed's Ben Smith, and Slate's Sasha Issenberg, I made the trek to Ben Cramer's home. John Harris, who runs Politico and is a mentor of mine, joked that our trip amounted to a young Bob Dylan going to visit his idol—Woody Guthrie—in a sanatorium in New Jersey as Guthrie was dying from Huntington's disease. It wasn't exactly like that—Ben Cramer is in fine health despite his steady cigar diet, and none of my quartet was an aspiring Dylan—but that gets at the idea.

As Jonathan's Jeep Cherokee pulled up to Ben Cramer's house we joked that it wouldn't be a huge shock if he came out of the house with a gun and shooed us off his property. After all, we had never met or spoken to the man—ever. Come out on his porch he did, but Ben Cramer was, blessedly, unarmed. We spent a sweltering summer night—the farmhouse is not air-conditioned—listening as Ben Cramer unspooled the story of *What It Takes,* from his nearly six-year effort of reporting and writing. For a bunch of young, ambitious political reporters, Ben Cramer was the word made flesh—the guy who had written the book that convinced us all (in some way) to become the journalists that sat in front of him that night. He signed our books—yes, we had lugged copies of *What It Takes* with us—saw us out, and urged us to call or write whenever the mood struck us. We swapped stories about Ben Cramer—he is rightly described as appealingly eccentric—all the way back to Washington, but I knew I wanted more. I wanted Ben Cramer one-on-one; I wanted to know what he was thinking—and why—when it came to *What It Takes*. I wanted to Ben Cramer Ben Cramer. Luckily he was willing.

> Joe Biden had balls. Lot of times, more balls than sense.
> This was from the jump—as a little kid.
>
> What he wanted it to feel like was the organized emotion
> of a football play—practiced for months, until it was
> clockwork—where he knew, where he *saw* in his mind,
> before the snap of the ball, how he'd run, exactly twenty
> yards down the field, where he'd feint for the goalpost and
> cut to the sideline, like it already *happened,* he saw how he'd
> plant his left foot . . . saw the tuft of grass that his cleats
> would dig into . . . the look on the cornerback's face . . .
> as he left (as he would leave) that sonofabitch *in the dust*!
>
> —Richard Ben Cramer on Joe Biden

When Ben Cramer came up with the idea of *What It Takes* he was thirty-five years old and living in New York City. He had done stints as a cops and obituaries writer with the *Baltimore Sun,* as a transportation correspondent, and as the *Philadelphia Inquirer*'s lone foreign correspondent, spending much of the late 1970s and early 1980s living in Egypt. (He got the gig because Robert McCartney, one of the senior correspondents from the paper, had just returned stateside when news broke that Israeli prime minister Menachem Begin would meet Egyptian president Anwar-Sadat on Christmas Day 1977. "I'm a Jew, I work on Christmas . . . I was the only gravy they got," recalled Ben Cramer.)

But he had an idea—an idea to answer that question that had been itching at the back of his mind in one way or another for decades. (Ben Cramer decided he wanted to be a reporter when he was eight years old; he was the editor of both his high school newspaper in upstate

New York and the one at Johns Hopkins University in Baltimore.) The idea, while compelling, was something short of fully formed. "I said, 'I don't know who the characters are, I don't know what the story is. Just give me several hundred thousand dollars and I'll see you in a few years and everything is going to be fine.' "

(His initial idea was to focus the book on Richard Nixon, who had been out of public life for more than a decade by that point. But his girlfriend at the time, who became his wife and, eventually, his ex-wife, vetoed the idea; "I am not living in a house where Nixon is living for three years," Ben Cramer recalls her saying.)

Remarkably, David Rosenthal—an editor at Random House who knew Ben Cramer's work from the magazine world (he had written well-regarded profiles of Ted Williams and Baltimore mayor William Donald Schaefer for *Esquire* in the early 1980s)—bit. ("I wouldn't have bought it," joked Ben Cramer.)

Ben Cramer moved from New York City to a house on Capitol Hill—Eighth Street, to be exact—in 1986 along with his researcher Mark Zwonitzer and immediately hit a brick wall in reporting. He started by calling the people whose names he read in the *Washington Post*, hoping to build relationships with the top people in campaigns. No one returned his calls. It went on like that for months, at which point Ben Cramer decided he needed either to do something very different or give up his dream of writing the next great campaign book.

He did something different. He flew to St. Louis and found Dick Gephardt's mother. (Gephardt was an up-and-comer in the House who would go on to win the Iowa caucuses but not much more in the 1988 presidential race.) He sat with her as she walked him through the family photo albums and told him all about the boy who had grown into the man who was running for president. "I had an absolute ball," said Ben Cramer, and in that moment, he knew he was on to something—a reporting approach that focused less on the candidate than on the people who had formed the candidate. "By the time I got back to [DC], I was not another schmuck with a notebook," said Ben Cramer. "I was his momma's friend, I had seen his uncle. He wanted to know how they were."

> With Gephardt, listening was a positive and physical act. You could *feel* him listening. It was not like, for instance, Biden, or [Michael] Dukakis, where listening was the absence of other action. (They weren't leaving, they weren't saying their next thing yet, so, therefore, they were still listening.) When Gephardt started to listen, his whole person went into "receive" mode. He locked his sky-blue eyes on your face, and they didn't wiggle around between your eyes and your mouth and the guy who walked in the door behind you: they were just on you, still and absorptive, like a couple of small blotters. Then, as you talked, his head cocked a bit, maybe twenty degrees off plumb, like that dog in the old RCA ad. Matter of fact, his face bore the same expression: that keen canine commingling of concern, curiosity, interest.
>
> —Richard Ben Cramer on Dick Gephardt

Over the next three and a half years—Ben Cramer reported in the book events taking place during all or part of 1986, 1987, 1988, and 1989—he took that same approach and methodically applied it to the other candidates, searching for the common thread that bound all of these men together.

That thread? Their mothers. "In every household the dad was in some way recessive," he said. "The moms took every bit of ambition and their focus and their will and pumped it into this kid until that little kid was running by the time he left that house."

That singular focus was not just from the candidates' mothers though. Ben Cramer said he was struck by how "their whole world bent around them . . . they were the heavy lumps of iron." That phe-nomenon also produced another one: the presidential candidates al-most always had, in Ben Cramer's words, "a crazy brother." Why? Because the golden child "sucks up every little bit of sunshine," leav-ing nothing for his siblings.

(Ben Cramer said he learned a reporting trick during those days that has served him well since: women make far better sources than men. "If you have a woman available to talk about somebody, why would you worry about any guys?" he says, adding that the women in the candidates' lives were the "greatest help to me.")

> Junior was the Roman Candle of the family, bright, hot,
> a sparkler—and likeliest to burn the fingers. He had
> all the old man's high spirits, but none of his taste for
> accommodation. In fact, he was more like Bar, the way he
> called a spade a spade. But it wasn't so easy for him to do it
> in the background, the way she'd done it all these years. No,
> he didn't mind being up front. But he'd learned some control
> as he'd neared the age of forty. In fact, these days, control,
> discipline—some of that old Bush medicine—was what he
> was always teaching himself.
>
> —Richard Ben Cramer on George W. Bush

By the time 1989 rolled around, Ben Cramer was still reporting a story than had ended a year before—George H. W. Bush won—and knew he had better start writing or run the risk of having the 1992 election overrun the story he had to tell. He moved to Cambridge, Maryland—about an hour south of where he currently lives—to write it. "I moved out of Washington because I didn't want it to sound like Washington," he recalls. It took him three years to produce the whole thing, a massive tome that ran more than 1,000 pages. (More on that in a minute.)

While Ben Cramer hawked the book every chance he got—he even got a few minutes of time on *Meet the Press*—sales were only so-so and the reviews were scathing. The *Boston Globe* referred to the book as *What It Weighs* for the better part of a decade. Maureen Dowd, writing in the *Washington Monthly*, bashed the book: "After reading every nuance, every shading, every interior monologue in this monster book, I can't say I've learned anything fundamentally new about any of the candidates," she wrote. But it was the *New York Times* review that still sticks in Ben Cramer's craw. It was written by a *Time* magazine campaign reporter named Laurence Barrett, who criticized the book as overly detailed and distracting. "What it takes to navigate *What It Takes* is great diligence and a tolerance of all manner of distracting mannerisms," wrote Barrett.

Ben Cramer, who acknowledges he went through a low period following the panning of the book, believes that the reaction was born of two realities. First, he "wrote most of the reporters up pretty harsh," casting them as intellectually indifferent men and women simply following whatever story the campaigns spoon-fed them. (Ben Cramer recalls with outrage—all these years later—that he was the lone reporter to go to Long Island to talk to Gephardt's brother, a professor at SUNY–Stony Brook, during the 1988 primary campaign.) Second, his approach to reporting—bottom up with a decidedly noncandidate focus—served as a challenge to the established order in Washington. "If I was right, they were wrong," Ben Cramer said about his reporting competitors. "Your stock and trade in DC is that you had [collected] wisdom and you are a part of that wisdom. If that wisdom is shown to be bankrupt, then what do you have?"

(One notable dissenter in the widespread negative reviews of *What It Takes* was Peggy Noonan, the speechwriter for Ronald Reagan and conservative pundit. Ben Cramer tells of a book party for *What It Takes* thrown by Si Newhouse, who owned Random House, during the 1992 Democratic National Convention at Billy's bar in New York City. Noonan "sweeps up to me and says 'Oh, Richard, I'm sorry I'm late. I had to finish it before I came. It's a masterpiece. They'll be reading it a hundred years from now.'" To which Newhouse replied, "They'll still be reading it a hundred years from now," recounts Ben Cramer with a cackle.)

The book never made money for Random House, but it did get Ben Cramer another book contract, which is what he was after in the first place. (He went on to write a very favorably reviewed biography of Yankee legend Joe DiMaggio, which came out in 2000.) And then something strange happened. Around the book's ten-year anniversary—2002 or thereabouts—it became, in Ben Cramer's words, a "magisterial classic." (That phrase, like much of Ben Cramer's patois, is said with tongue firmly planted in cheek.)

For me—and for my generation of political journalists—the book spoke to something elemental about why we were drawn to the field. It tried like hell to get at who these people, who were arrogant enough to believe they among all others in the country should represent us in the White House, were before they ever became bold-faced names. It tried to connect what they once were to who they became. It was a fundamental reimagining of how campaigns, and the candidates who populated them, could be covered. Rather than focusing on what they said, *What It Takes* focused on why they said it—not by asking the candidates but by asking the people who helped forge the personalities of the candidates so long ago.

Ben Cramer ascribes the remarkable second life of the book to the fact that the younger generation was not "personally threatened" by what the book said. "As the older people have gone on to be in think tanks and PR for their local water utility companies, the young people's idea of it has prevailed gradually," he says with not a little bit of self-satisfaction. "I am very pleased with their reaction to it."

In the end, *What It Takes* did what Ben Cramer imagined it could do twenty-five years ago. He zigged when everyone else zagged and produced a book that told a richer, more enlightening story of the campaign than anyone produced that year or has in any year since.

"My goal was always to hear somebody tell what I had written to somebody else in the morning in an elevator," he said. "If I could get somebody to tell that story again, I'd won."

Yes, he had.

## THE FIX'S FIVE MUST-READ WASHINGTON BOOKS

If you could read only five books in order to understand how Washington works, these would be the five.

### 1. *What It Takes* by Richard Ben Cramer

Simply put: the book to which all other campaign books will be compared. Cramer's book has aged well, with his detailed portraits of men who stayed in the public limelight—George W. Bush (he was heavily involved in his dad's 1988 race), Dick Gephardt, Joe Biden— long after the 1988 campaign ended. No other book, before or since, takes you so far inside the psyches of the kind of people who decide to run for president. Ben Cramer's takes on these men can be cutting but are almost always sympathetic in some way—as we are all able to see a bit of ourselves reflected in them.

### 2. *The Ambition and the Power* by John M. Barry

This is a book that simply could not be produced today. Barry was granted unbelievable access to the major players in House politics and, as a result, delivers a front-row-seat view of the collapse of then House Speaker Jim Wright. He also captures the essence of the man masterminding the overthrow of Wright—none other than then little-known Georgia congressman Newt Gingrich. If ever you wanted a look into how House politics really works, this is the book.

**3. *Game Change: Obama and the Clintons, McCain and Palin, and the Race of a Lifetime* by John Heilemann and Mark Halperin**

Ever wondered what it would be like if campaigns were covered and written about as the soap operas that they are? *Game Change*, Heilemann and Halperin's chronicle of the 2008 presidential campaign, answered that question. The answer? Damn entertaining. The book was chock-full of revelations—Senate Majority Leader Harry Reid saying Obama had no noticeable "Negro dialect"—and read more like a romance novel than the traditional campaign blow-by-blows. Its depiction of Elizabeth and John Edwards—as shallow and callow political actors interested in settling scores as much as in leading the nation—was one of the most devastating (and accurate) pieces of campaign journalism on record. So salacious was the book that it was turned into a movie by—who else?—HBO in the spring of 2012. Julianne Moore played Sarah Palin. 'Nuff said.

**4. *Path to Power / Means of Ascent / Master of the Senate / The Passage of Power* by Robert Caro**

Yes, Caro has been at work on this tetralogy of books about President Lyndon Johnson for the better part of the last three decades. (The fourth book, dealing with Johnson's ascension to the White House, came out in May 2012.) But there is no political biography as compelling as that of Johnson, as told through Caro's words. Johnson's path to power, which, coincidentally, is the title of the first book in the series, encapsulates the ambition, drive, and insecurity present in almost every truly great politician.

**5. *Primary Colors* by Joe Klein**

The only piece of fiction on our list isn't even really fiction. Originally touted as a novel by an anonymous author, the book deals with a talented but fatally flawed southern governor seeking the presidency in the early 1990s. (Sound like anyone you might know?) Klein, a reporter at *Newsweek* at the time, denied his authorship for the better part of four years even as *Primary Colors* enjoyed considerable commercial and critical success. (In 1996 he eventually admitted he had written the book.) Regardless of the dispute over who wrote it, the book is as good a window into Clinton's mind as you will find anywhere.

And here's my extended list of the best political fiction and nonfiction, which was compiled with the help of suggestions from Fix readers across the country.

### FICTION
*Jack Gance* by Ward Just
*The Wanting of Levine* by Michael Halberstam
*The People's Choice* by Jeff Greenfield
*The Last Hurrah* by Edwin O'Connor
*The Shad Treatment* by Garrett Epps
*The Woody* by Peter Lefcourt
*The Ninth Wave* by Eugene Burdick
*Advise and Consent* by Allen Drury
*The Gay Place* by William Brammer
*Thank You for Smoking* by Christopher Buckley
*Seven Days in May* by Fletcher Knebel and Charles Bailey
*Lincoln* by Gore Vidal

### NONFICTION
*The Power Broker* by Robert Caro
*The Survivor: Bill Clinton in the White House* by John F. Harris
*The Politicos* by Matthew Josephson
*Politician* by Ronnie Dugger
*Rules for Radicals* by Saul Alinsky
*City for Sale* by Jack Newfield and Wayne Barrett

*Who Governs* by Robert Dahl

*Boys on the Bus* by Tim Crouse

*The Prince* by Machiavelli

*Huey Long* by T. Harry Williams

*Earl of Louisiana* by A. J. Liebling

*Southern Politics in State and Nation* by V. O. Key

*Hardball* by Chris Matthews

*The Power Game* by Hedrick Smith

*Man of the House* by Tip O'Neill

*Nixonland* by Rick Perlstein

*The Selling of the President* by Joe McGinnis

*What I Saw at the Revolution* by Peggy Noonan

*Enduring Revolution* by Major Garrett

*Boss* by Mike Royko

*Bad Boy: The Life and Politics of Lee Atwater* by John Brady

*Bare Knuckles and Back Rooms* by Ed Rollins

*RFK* by Jack Newfield

*Lyndon Johnson and the American Dream*
    by Doris Kearns Goodwin

*Fear and Loathing on the Campaign Trail*
    by Hunter S. Thompson

*When Hell Froze Over* by Dwayne Yancey

*The Making of the President 1960* by Theodore White

*The Future of American Politics* by Samuel Lubell

*The Real Majority: The Classic Examination of the American
    Electorate* by Ben Wattenberg and Richard Scammon

*Conscience of a Conservative* by Barry Goldwater

*The Last Hayride* by John Maginnis

*Politics Lost* by Joe Klein

*Marathon* by Jules Witcover

*Truman* by David McCullough

*President Reagan: The Role of a Lifetime* by Lou Cannon

*The Best and the Brightest* by David Halbertsam
*Wallace* by Marshall Frady
*Lincoln* by David Herbert Donald
*1912: Wilson, Roosevelt, Taft and Debs—the Election That
    Changed the Country* by James Chace

And, while we're at it, here are the best political movies of all time:

*Absolute Power*
*Advise and Consent*
*All the King's Men*
*All the President's Men*
*The American President*
*Being There*
*The Best Man*
*Blaze*
*Bob Roberts*
*Boogie Man: The Lee Atwater Story*
*Bulworth*
*The Candidate*
*Charlie Wilson's War*
*The Contender*
*Dave*
*The Distinguished Gentleman*
*Dr. Strangelove*
*Duck Soup*
*Election*
*Frost/Nixon*
*In the Loop*
*Journeys with George*
*The Man Who Shot Liberty Valance*
*The Manchurian Candidate*

*Mr. Smith Goes to Washington*
*My Fellow Americans*
*Nashville*
*Nixon*
*O Brother, Where Art Thou?*
*Our Brand Is Crisis*
*A Perfect Candidate*
*Power*
*Primary Colors*
*Recount*
*Seven Days in May*
*State of the Union*
*Street Fight*
*Taking on the Kennedys*
*Thirteen Days*
*Thank You for Smoking*
*True Colors*
*Truman*
*Vote for Me*
*Wag the Dog*
*The War Room*

# THE TEN BEST/WORST NEGATIVE ADS IN POLITICAL HISTORY

Everyone hates negative television ads. They play to our worst instincts, amount to lowest-common-denominator politics, and, often, distort—or just outright destroy—a candidate's record. They also work, which is why so many of them are run in every high-profile campaign. (In the 2012 Florida Republican primary 92 percent of the ads were negative—a stunning figure, which speaks to their efficacy.)

Voters might not like negative ads but they tend to factor the information provided in them into their decision-making process. I'll never forget going home to Connecticut—yeah, Nutmeg State!—to cover the 2006 primary fight between Senator Joe Lieberman (I), who had pissed the entire Democratic Party off with his support for the war in Iraq, and cable television magnate (awesome job description) Ned Lamont. Sensing the race was slipping from him, Lieberman went on the attack—hard—with ads pointing out that Lamont had often sided with the Republican members of the Greenwich board of selectmen.

In a conversation with my dad—not a terribly political guy but someone who pays attention to the news—he casually mentioned Lamont's siding with Republicans in those votes. He didn't say he had seen it in a TV ad; he didn't say he had seen it anywhere. But I knew he had gotten that piece of information straight from Lieberman's negative attack. Lamont went on to win the primary—though I am still not sure whom my dad voted for—but that moment proved a point to me: negative ads work, no matter what voters say about them not working. They insinuate themselves into your political consciousness, and when you go to the voting booth, they are the voice whispering in the back of your head. You may not always listen to that niggling voice, but you know it's there.

Given how powerful negative ads are, it's worth revisiting some of the greatest—or worst, depending on how you view things—negative television ads in political history. Remember that television ads date back only to 1952, which gives me a relatively limited sample from which to choose. (I would have killed to have TV ads during the Thomas Jefferson–John Adams race in 1800. Those negative ads would have been fierce!)

My all-time favorite negative ads—the ones you can refer to with a word or a single phrase and political types know exactly what you are talking about—are below. They are ranked in order of their fame/infamy.

## DAISY

[http://www.youtube.com/watch?v=ExjDzDsgbww]: The granddaddy of them all, this ad ran only one time—in September on NBC during a showing of *David and Bathsheba* with Gregory Peck—during the 1964 presidential campaign. Sponsored by Lyndon Johnson, it featured a little girl—her name was Monique Luiz—plucking petals off a daisy and counting. (The ad's official title was "Peace Little Girl.") A narrator's foreboding voice picked up the countdown as the camera zoomed in on the girl's face. As the narrator reached "zero" a nuclear explosion filled the screen. "These are the stakes," said the narrator. "To make a world in which all of God's children can live or to go into the dark. We must love one another or we must die." Yes, that is the real text of the ad.

The commercial never mentioned Republican presidential candidate Barry Goldwater by name, but it didn't have to. At a time of considerable anxiety about nuclear war, Johnson's ad made the not-so-subtle suggestion that Goldwater was just not someone who could be trusted to have his finger on the button. (Did that button actually exist? If so, I hope you couldn't just accidentally brush up against it.)

The ad was remarkable for several reasons—both obvious and not. It amounted to the first negative ad in political campaign history, the one to which every other ad would be compared. But it also marked the first presidential campaign in which a commercial ad agency—Doyle Dane Bernbach, who cut spots for Volkswagen among others—was employed in a presidential campaign. "It wasn't advertising like we think of advertising today," Bob Mann, who wrote an entire book on the ad entitled *Daisy Petals and Mushroom Clouds: LBJ, Barry Goldwater, and the Ad That Changed American Politics,* said on a panel about the ad in the fall of 2011.

While the ad is generally credited with destroying Goldwater's chances, that analysis skips over a crucial point: Goldwater never had any chance to beat Johnson. The ad's impact then is in what it presaged, not in what it meant at the moment.

## WILLIE HORTON

[http://www.youtube.com/watch?v=EC9j6Wfdq3o]: This ad, which was run by something called the National Security PAC during the

1988 campaign, still evokes strong emotions—and a fierce debate about race in politics—more than twenty years after it aired.

The goal of the ad, which was written and conceived of by a man named Floyd Brown, was simple: to cast Massachusetts governor Michael Dukakis, the Democratic presidential nominee, as weak on crime. The chosen weapon to do so was a man named Willie Horton, a man imprisoned for first-degree murder in Massachusetts who escaped while on a weekend furlough—a program supported by Dukakis. After more than a year on the lam, Horton beat a Maryland couple, stabbing the man and raping the woman.

The picture of Horton shown on screen was of an African American man with a thick goatee and an Afro—a visual that Democrats then (and to this day) insisted was aimed at scaring suburban white voters about what might happen in their neighborhoods under a Dukakis presidency. (The ad was shot in black and white, making Horton seem all the more menacing. "They ran my ads in black and white because it was a black-and-white campaign," the incarcerated Horton told legendary *Newsday* columnist Jimmy Breslin in 1989.)

Earlier in the campaign, Lee Atwater, who managed George H. W. Bush's campaign, had pledged to "make Willie Horton so famous, people will think he's on the ticket." That's exactly what happened. Dukakis and Horton became inextricably linked in voters' minds, an image that led to the Massachusetts governor's defeat.

## "ANY QUESTIONS"

[http://www.youtube.com/watch?v=V4Zk9YmED48]: When Democrats chose Massachusetts senator John Kerry as their party's nominee in 2004, his military record—he had been awarded a Bronze Star for his service in Vietnam—was regarded as his greatest strength in a campaign expected to revolve around military might. (The country, still reeling from the attacks of September 11, 2011, was in the midst of wars in Afghanistan and Iraq.)

And so, no one—including Kerry—paid much attention when a group calling themselves Swift Boat Veterans for Truth formed in May 2004. That all changed when, in August of that year, SBVT launched this ad, which featured testimonials from a number of men who had served with Kerry alleging that he had either fudged or downright lied about a number of his accomplishments in Vietnam. The minute-long commercial, which featured the likes of Lieutenant Commander George Elliott insisting that "John Kerry has not been honest" about Vietnam, was a devastating series of body blows to the Massachusetts Democrat's campaign.

Kerry and his campaign team continued to ignore the commercials under the (false) belief that voters would see them for what they were: ax grinding by a relatively small group of men who didn't like what Kerry had done after the war. (There were reports that he had thrown away several of his medals of valor during antiwar protests, although Kerry denied he had ever done so.)

By the time Kerry realized what was happening it was already too late. The SBVT ads had taken a perceived strength for the Democrat and turned it into a weakness. Doubt had been planted in voters' minds about how valorous Kerry's service in Vietnam actually was; if he was fibbing about that, voters wondered, what else might he be telling less than the whole truth about? It was plenty of doubt to sink Kerry's chances, despite Bush's unpopularity and the growing unpopularity of the war in Iraq. So damaging were the ads that a new verb was coined for the drive-by demolition of politicians by outside groups: *swiftboating.*

## THE BEAR

[http://www.youtube.com/watch?v=NpwdcmjBgNA]: The ad, run by President Ronald Reagan as he sought a second term in 1984, is simultaneously one of the oddest and most effective negative ads ever. As the title suggests, the star of the ad is a bear who wanders around a mountainside while a narrator, advertising exec Hal Riney, says: "There is a bear in the woods. For some people the bear is easy to see. Some people don't see it at all. Some people say the bear is tame, others say it's vicious and dangerous." The bear is shown confronting a man as the narrator asks: "Since no one can really be sure, isn't it smart to be as strong as the bear? If there is a bear?" The words "President Reagan: Prepared for Peace" appear on the screen as the ad ends.

The bear, in case you missed it (and lots of people in focus groups did), represents the Soviet Union. The ad was designed to make the case that Reagan's trust-but-verify approach to the USSR was a safer bet than the more welcoming posture toward Russia adopted by Minnesota senator Walter Mondale, the Democratic presidential nominee.

Judging just how effective the "bear ad" actually was is difficult because by the time Reagan's campaign aired it, the incumbent was well on his way to the forty-nine-state victory he racked up on election day 1984. What's less debatable is the ad's place in campaign lore and its influence on the ad makers who followed in Riney's footsteps. During the 2004 campaign, Bush adman Mark McKinnon produced an ad entitled "Wolves" that showed the animals prowling through a dense forest while a narrator said: "Weakness attracts those who are waiting to do America harm."

## 3 AM PHONE CALL

[http://www.youtube.com/watch?v=7yr7odFUARg]: For months, Hillary Rodham Clinton's 2008 presidential campaign had looked unsuccessfully for a way to capture the lingering doubts some voters had about nominating the decidedly inexperienced Barack Obama as their standard-bearer in the race for the White House.

This ad, produced by Mandy Grunwald and conceptualized by pollster and chief strategist Mark Penn, did the trick. The sound of a ringing phone was laid over images of children asleep as a narrator said: "It's 3 AM and your children are safe and asleep. But there's a phone in the White House and it's ringing. Something is happening in the world. Your vote will decide who answers that call."

The commercial goes on to suggest that you want "someone who already knows the world's leaders, knows the military, someone tested and ready to lead in a dangerous world" picking up that call. While neither Clinton nor Obama is named in the bulk of the ad, the message to voters was perfectly clear: Obama may sound and look good, but he simply hasn't been tested (and passed) in the way Clinton has.

The ad sparked a running debate in the Democratic primary over the candidates' readiness and preparedness for office. Obama responded with his own commercial that mirrored the sleeping children and ringing phone of the Clinton ad but went on to note that the Illinois senator was "the only one who had the judgment and courage to oppose the Iraq war from the start." Clinton's ad didn't win her the nomination—Obama's delegate lead was already too large for a single ad or message to change—but it is almost certainly responsible for her victories in the early March primaries in Ohio and Texas, wins that allowed her to remain in the race for the duration.

## "IN HIS OWN WORDS"

[http://www.youtube.com/watch?v=CrDZ_Jt_KOS]: Run by former Republican representative John Thune in his 2004 upset victory over Senate Majority Leader Tom Daschle, this ad ushered in a new era of negative advertising that still reigns supreme today: using a candidate's own words against him.

Daschle had represented South Dakota since 1986, winning in a Republican-leaning state because of his ability to make the case that regardless of which party he aligned himself with, he always had the best interests of South Dakotans at heart. This ad, which was produced by Thune media consultant Scott Howell, changed all that by splicing a series of video clips from Daschle together that painted him as a liberal Democrat loyal, first and foremost, to his party in Washington. "I want to thank you for sending Hillary Clinton to Washington to represent you," Daschle said in one clip. "No one does it better." In another Daschle pledges not to "surrender sacred ground . . . and that includes a woman's constitutional right to choose." Oomph.

Daschle insisted the quotes had been taken out of context, but the damage was very much done. Instead of being "our Tom Daschle," the ad had transformed him into "the Democrats' Tom Daschle," a losing recipe for a Democrat seeking reelection in GOP-friendly territory in 2004. Thune won narrowly, the first candidate to defeat a sitting Senate majority leader in fifty-two (!) years.

The lesson that campaigns—Democratic and Republican—learned from the "In His Own Words" ad was simple yet profound: voters tended to dismiss the run-of-the-mill negative commercial with a grainy picture of your opponent and foreboding music. But if that same opponent could be found saying something incriminating, embarrassing, or just plain dumb, then you were (and are) on to something.

## MONTANA BEAUTY PARLOR

[http://www.youtube.com/watch?v=SAnzfcWC6Tk]:   Ostensibly this commercial for Montana senator Max Baucus's (D) 2002 campaign was designed to bring to light allegations of tax fraud against his opponent, a state senator named Mike Taylor. But that's like saying Cirque du Soleil is a tumbling act.

Democrats in the state had unearthed old video footage of Taylor applying cream and rubbing another man's temples—all while dressed in the worst of the early 1980s fashion. (Prior to being elected to the state senate Taylor ran a beauty salon. A Democratic opposition researcher actually found the tape while combing through the video archives of a Colorado public television station.) The ad's closing line said it all: "Mike Taylor, not the way we do business in Montana." (So famous was the ad that *Rock Center*—NBC's news magazine show—featured it as part of a piece on opposition research in March 2012.)

Taylor dropped from the race shortly after the ad began airing, insisting Democrats had smeared him by insinuating in the ad that he was gay. Standing with his wife—not accidental—Taylor said, "My opponent's lies about me are hurting my wife, my family, my friends, my party, and most of all, Montanans from all walks of life." Democrats played dumb, arguing that the ad was simply taking note of the $159,000 Taylor had received from a student loan program and diverted to his own personal accounts.

Taylor, oddly, got back into the race in its final weeks but was a relative nonfactor as Baucus cruised to a fifth term that November.

## TANK

[http://www.youtube.com/watch?v=9LyYD166ync]: A disastrous photo op of Dukakis riding around in a tank during a tour of a General Dynamics plant in Michigan was turned into a brilliantly cutting spot by the George H. W. Bush ad team.

Dukakis's visit to the plant—and his decision to don a helmet and ride around in a tank—was aimed at debunking the idea that he was too soft to be the nation's commander in chief. It accomplished the exact opposite. Dukakis looked as if he had never worn a helmet or been in a tank before—for good reason, since he hadn't—and became a figure of derision, not strength.

In the Bush ad, the tank is shown driving while a narrator details the fact that "Michael Dukakis has opposed nearly every defense system we developed." The ad ends with a close-up of Dukakis—helmet and all—in the tank as the narrator says: "Now he wants to be our commander in chief . . . America can't afford that risk."

In later years, Dukakis insisted that the tank ad (or the Willie Horton ad) could have been weathered if he had run a better general election campaign. Maybe. But so lasting is the image of Dukakis in the tank that Newt Gingrich referenced it during the 2012 New Hampshire Republican primary. At a stop at a tank museum in Wolfeboro, Gingrich said, "I look at this tank lovingly because I remember Michael Dukakis," as the crowd laughed in knowing ridicule. Added Gingrich: "Governors of Massachusetts don't always make good presidential candidates."

## WINDSURFING

[http://www.youtube.com/watch?v=pbdzMLk9wHQ]: If a picture is worth a thousand words, who knows how much a video of your opponent windsurfing is worth in a presidential campaign.

In the 2004 race, President George W. Bush had just such footage of John Kerry, his Democratic opponent. With the "Blue Danube Waltz" by Johann Strauss as the soundtrack, Bush adman Mark McKinnon ran a series of images of Kerry windsurfing to and fro as a visual representation of the alleged flip-flops in the Massachusetts senator's voting record. "Kerry voted for the Iraq war, opposed it, supported it, and now opposes it again." (For each switch of position, Kerry was shown windsurfing in opposite directions.) "John Kerry, whichever way the wind blows," said the ad's narrator at the conclusion of the ad's thirty seconds.

Not only did the commercial use a powerful visual to drive home the idea that Kerry had taken a series of seemingly contradictory positions, but it also made sure people knew that the Democratic nominee liked to windsurf—a hobby the average American has neither the money nor the inclination to pursue.

It was a double whammy that helped sink Kerry.

## ECHO

[http://www.youtube.com/watch?v=sw_0a54S8po]: When eBay executive Meg Whitman ran for governor of California in 2010, she pitched herself as something the state had never seen before: a successful businesswoman ready, willing, and able to bring the lessons she had learned in the private sector to bear on the Golden State's mounting list of problems.

That pitch was working right up until state attorney general Jerry Brown's campaign launched this ad, which spliced Whitman's rhetoric with that of unpopular outgoing governor Arnold Schwarzenegger and found a near-perfect match. "We do not have a revenue problem, we have a spending problem," said Schwarzenegger. "We do not have a revenue problem, we have a spending problem," said Whitman. "Jobs, jobs, jobs," says Schwarzenegger. "Jobs, jobs, jobs," says Whitman. You get the idea. But, in case you didn't, the ad ends with a line from a *San Jose Mercury News* op-ed: "We tried that. It didn't work."

Whitman went from something new and appealing to something old and predictable in sixty seconds. She was never able to change that image and went down to a huge defeat even as she dumped upwards of $100 million of her own money on the race.

What does that prove? That a compelling message trumps lots and lots of cash any day.

*Honorable Mention*

## THE ROSS PEROT INFOMERCIALS

It's impossible to do a list of the best/worst of any political advertising and not include these infomercials that the Texas billionaire funded during his 1992 independent bid for president. Perot wanted to make sure people knew he wasn't just the same old sort of politician who runs for president. And boy oh boy did he do that.

Perot took on a sort of populist scold/encouraging teacher persona in the infomercials as he tried to use them as a way to educate the public on the problems created by the crushing national debt. (Sound familiar?) Perot used any number of charts (and more charts!) and graphs to illustrate that point as well as a "voodoo stick" (not kidding) that doubled as his pointer.

The infomercials felt a little like a policy version of the "Wayne's World" skit on *Saturday Night Live*. They were certainly different. But a little too different for the American public.

# CONGRESS DOESN'T WORK. HERE ARE FIVE IDEAS ON HOW IT COULD

The American public hates Congress. Like, really hates it. For all of 2011, Congress averaged a 17 percent approval rating in Gallup's weekly polling, the lowest ever recorded by that organization. That made the establishment roughly as popular as Paris Hilton (15 percent approval), BP during the Gulf Coast oil spill (16 percent), and the idea of the United States turning into a Communist country (11 percent). So, not good.

Many political cynics—and they are legion—insist that Congress has always been an unpopular institution and will forever remain one. True. But that misses the point that things are measurably and objectively worse now than they ever have been before. The public used to dislike Congress as an institution but defend the relative merits of their own individual members. In recent years, the gap between those two numbers has narrowed as people's disenchantment with the body writ large has begun to infect even the most beloved members.

Take the fight over raising the debt ceiling, a debate that paralyzed official Washington for the entirety of the spring and summer of 2011. The limit on the nation's credit card had regularly been raised in the past—seventy-four times since 1962 to be exact—but newly elected Republican members aligned with the Tea Party insisted that the days of writing checks that their collective asses couldn't cash would come to an end this time around. (Gross imagery, I know.)

As the country teetered on the verge of default, Congress twiddled their thumbs—seemingly daring the financial world to call their bluff. Standard & Poor's did, downgrading the U.S.'s credit rating for the first time in history. (We made history! Wait . . .) A deal was finally struck that averted default and created a super committee—irony intended—that was supposed to figure things out. Except that they didn't. Can you blame people for thinking Congress was the appendix of the body politic, a part that was there but no one really knew why?

The damage to Congress's already terrible reputation was significant. Republican pollster Bill McInturff wrote a memo in the immediate aftermath of the debt ceiling "deal," trying to put it into some political context. "The debt ceiling negotiation is an extremely significant event that is profoundly and sharply reshaping views of the economy and the federal government," wrote McInturff. "It has led to a scary erosion in confidence in both, at a time when this steep drop in confidence can be least afforded." He added: "The perception of how Washington handled the debt ceiling negotiation led to an immediate collapse of confidence in government and all the major players, including President Obama and Republicans in Congress."

Just in case you need more evidence of this pox on both your houses (of Congress) mentality, all you need to do is check out this word cloud derived from a *Washington Post*–Pew poll where respondents were asked to say the first word that came to mind. The three most commonly mentioned words? *Stupid, ridiculous*, and *disgusting*. That about covers it.

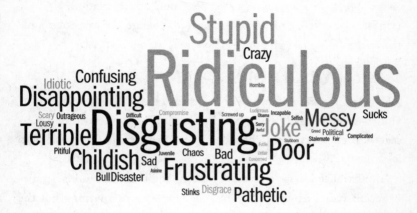

The inability of Congress to do much of anything stems from a variety of causes. The bases of the two parties are further apart ideologically than they have ever been before. (Gallup polling for 2009, 2010, and 2011 shows that the gap between Republicans and Democrats regarding how President Obama is doing his job is wider than *any* first three years of *any* president on record.) A permanent election mentality has seized Washington, driven largely by the prohibitive cost of running for reelection; it takes so much money to run and win that incumbents spend hours a day raising money almost from the moment they are elected to office. And over the past decade a surprisingly large number of House members—twenty to be exact—have been elected to the Senate and have brought the more confrontational and less bipartisan approach that dominates the lower chamber to the world's greatest deliberative body.

Political scientists have written books—and will continue to write books—about why Congress has stopped functioning anywhere close to how the Founders would have imagined it. But I am all about solutions—winning the future!—and below offer five (relatively) quick fixes for Congress's current problems. You'll notice most of these suggested solutions focus on elections, not legislation, a reflection of the fact that I believe you have to change the kind of people who get to Congress before you can change Congress.

## 1. FOUR-YEAR HOUSE TERMS

The current system of two-year terms for House members is equivalent to watching half of a movie. By the time you've settled into your seat, figured out who the characters are, and sussed out the basic plot, it's time to go.

And because House races have become multi-million-dollar affairs in recent years, newly elected members who sit in anything but the safest of congressional districts spend the vast majority of their first two years in office raising money in the hopes of making it to a second term. That, surprisingly enough, isn't conducive to actual legislative achievement.

Extending House terms to four years—the same period of time presidents, governors, and other statewide elected officials serve—would slow the dash for cash slightly and allow freshman lawmakers some chance to actually think about what they want to do—other than be reelected—with the seat they hold.

Even if House terms were doubled to four years, it would still make them two years short of the Senate's six-year terms—preserving the divide between a body more receptive to the will of the people and one that prides itself on being the more temperate, slower-moving body.

A possible wrinkle: split up the House between those members in competitive districts and those who aren't. Make anyone who sits in a district where the last presidential nominee of his party got 60 percent of the vote or more run every two years, forcing him to stay vigilant, in case someone within his own party wants to challenge him in a primary. (The simple truth is that members who sit in safe districts are almost entirely free of public accountability at this point. Voters don't pay all that much attention to what their specific House member is doing unless the incumbent in these districts commits a crime. Literally. So House members are likely to get reelected thanks to a money edge and the other advantages of incumbency.)

Give the members who sit in seats where their party's presidential nominee won less than 60 percent four years to make their mark. They're the ones who really need the extra time to try to show voters in their swing districts why they deserve a second term.

An added bonus of that approach for political junkies: running up the score might be a disincentive in such a system. Members might shoot to win 59 percent of the vote in order to double their amount of time in office. But that also could be playing with fire, as running to keep it close could backfire if you got caught in a last-minute wave or made some sort of major gaffe in the final weeks of a campaign. Oh man, that would be awesome. Admit it. It would rock.

## 2. NONPARTISAN REDISTRICTING

Every ten years, each state redraws its congressional lines. How these lines are drawn—and by whom—can make a decade-long difference in the competitiveness of a single state. Unfortunately a majority of states still allow some combination of the state legislature and/or governor to draw the lines—a reality that not only makes the process decidedly partisan but also de-emphasizes the sort of compromise-minded politics that Congress needs more of.

Take California. In 2001, Democrats—John Burton, the state senate president, and Michael Berman, the brother of California representative Howard Berman, to be exact—controlled all the levers of the process and set about protecting their large majority in the massive fifty-three-person delegation. Republican incumbents went along for the ride, content with holding the seats they had with no real prospects of picking up any new territory over the decade. (The one incumbent who got shafted was Democrat Gary Condit, who at the time was fending off allegations that he might have killed his onetime lover Chandra Levy. Democrats made his district more Democratic and he lost in the 2002 primary.) The result of the deal cut by both parties' incumbents? One of the fifty-three—yes, *fifty-three*—congressional districts changed party control over the entire decade of the 2000s. (That was Representative Richard Pombo, a Republican, who lost a race to Jerry McNerney in 2008.)

That lack of competitiveness drove Governor Arnold Schwarzenegger to push a ballot measure that would take power for drawing congressional lines away from the legislature and put it in the hands of a so-called citizens commission—a group of allegedly average people who would craft the lines without any political considerations or allegiances. Proposition 11, as the measure was known, passed with 51 percent of the vote in November 2008, and the citizens commission redrew California's map in 2011. The result? Thirteen districts rated as competitive heading into November by the Cook Political Report, a nonpartisan political handicapping shop (and my first employer out of college!). Thirteen out of fifty-three is still less than 25 percent of all the California congressional seats, but it's at least a step in the right direction.

The problem is that California's citizens redistricting commission is the exception, not the rule. It is one of only seven states—Washington, Oregon, Idaho, Hawaii, Iowa, and New Jersey are the others—that employ some sort of nonpartisan method of drawing lines. The other forty-three states still use the mostly or purely partisan approach, in which the relative competitiveness of a state for a decade is determined by which party controls the governorship and the state legislature.

It's ridiculous. I mean, in what other line of work do you get to determine—for a decade, no less—the relative safety of your job? "Um, yes, boss, I've done a good job. I should get a ten-year guaranteed contract with no option for you to get out of it—no matter how poor a job I do." It makes no sense, and it needs to stop.

Nonpartisan redistricting commissions in every state would likely double—and maybe triple—the number of genuinely competitive races in the country. (Look at Iowa, which draws its lines by commission; the state has four congressional districts, each of which is considered at least marginally competitive heading into November.)

That level of competitiveness would put a premium on candidates who were not simply water carriers for one party base or the other but rather messengers to the ideological middle, where elections are won and lost. And once they got to Washington, they would know that simply retreating into an ideological corner would ensure their defeat when they next stood for election.

Congressional redistricting might happen only once a decade, but its impact is vast. Change how lines get drawn and you change who gets elected—and how they act once they win.

## 3. OPEN PRIMARIES

In the majority of states in the country, the only people who can vote in a primary are those registered as members of the party—a "closed primary" system in the nomenclature of elections. For Republicans, thirty-one states have primaries that are either closed or semiclosed, which means that independents can vote. That number is twenty-nine states for Democrats.

The goal of closed primaries is a simple one: candidates should be picked by people who have a demonstrated commitment to a party, not by fly-by-nighters who may or may not have any long-term dedication to one side or the other. The other argument in favor of closed primaries is that it wards off the other side meddling in a primary in hopes of nominating the weaker candidate for the general election. The most famous example of that phenomenon was conservative talk radio host Rush Limbaugh's "Operation Chaos" in which he urged listeners to cross over and cast votes for Senator Hillary Rodham Clinton's 2008 presidential bid in hopes of extending the race between the former first lady and then Illinois senator Barack Obama. The primaries did go on—and on—all the way through June 6, but there was no empirical evidence that Limbaugh had swayed enough Republican voters to claim credit for the lengthening of the Democratic race.

What closed primaries produce—and there is plenty of empirical evidence here—is candidates who appeal to the hardest liners of each party. And while that's fine in some places—conservative districts having conservative representation makes sense after all—it's not the right system for the majority of districts and states in the country. After all, if you are elected thanks to your strict adherence to the principles lovingly cradled by the Democratic base, what incentive do you have to do anything in a bipartisan manner once you get to Washington?

Imagine if all fifty states had open primaries where voters were free to vote in whichever primary they were more interested or invested in. While Republicans would almost certainly vote in large numbers in Republican primaries (and Democrats in Democratic primaries), candidates would be forced to moderate their messaging—at least somewhat—in hopes of appealing to the independents and crossover voters looking to make up their minds.

A more centrist—or at least ideologically diverse—electorate would also encourage more moderate-minded candidates that they might be able to win. Take Tom Davis. In 2008 Davis, a proven vote-getting centrist Republican, was considering a run for an open Senate seat in Virginia. But Virginia Republicans decided to choose their nominee via a convention process—in which 3,500 or so hard-core GOPers would pick the candidate—rather than a primary. Davis, knowing his moderate views would make him anathema to that crowd, bowed out in favor of former governor Jim Gilmore, a conservative but someone with little appeal to the middle of the electorate. Gilmore won the convention easily and then, predictably, was swamped in the general election by Democrat Mark Warner.

If the Tom Davises of the world had the chance to run in open primaries, a lot more of them would. And while not all of them would win—Davis would likely have come up short against the popular Warner too—some would. And electing centrists to the House and Senate would provide an incentive for deal making, the sort of thing that is currently nonexistent.

## 4. MAKE TERM LIMITS REAL

In the 1990s, term limits were all the rage. Hoping to convince the public that they didn't want to make a living out of being in politics, candidates across the country—from the state legislature all the way up to the House and Senate—signed a pledge from U.S. Term Limits, an independent organization, committing themselves to spend only two terms in the Senate or three terms in the House.

But when those pledges came due, many of the reform-minded politicians balked. They liked being in office. They felt like building seniority was good for their constituents, not bad. They wouldn't have ever signed the pledge if they knew then what they know now, they argued. The term-limits community, not surprisingly, wasn't happy—and vowed to exact revenge.

The test case was Washington representative George Nethercutt (R), who had ousted Speaker of the House Tom Foley (D) in 1994 largely by casting his opponent as an out-of-touch career politician. Six years later when it came time to honor his term-limit pledge, however, Nethercutt decided he'd rather not. The term-limits crowd went at him *hard*—and lost. Without a demonstrated ability to punish those who would cross them, the term-limits movement withered. After all, empty threats don't scare anyone.

The failure of term limits to flex its political muscle doesn't mean, however, that it's a bad idea. Just that the term-limits folks went about it the wrong way. (After all, there are term limits in eight state legislatures, and thirty-seven states have term limits for their statewide elected officials.) In order to have real bite, term limits need to be written into the law, which is, in the case of the U.S. Congress, the Constitution.

Would some elected officials balk? Absolutely. But standing against the idea of a citizen legislature in an America where people hate politicians and everything associated with them is a recipe for disaster. Public pressure and a fear of losing on this one issue would likely convince some of the on-the-fence members to get behind the bill.

Our suggested term limits? Six terms for a House member and two terms for a senator. That makes it an equal twelve years on both sides of the Capitol. It's enough time so that you aren't out of office as soon as you actually begin to figure out how the place works. And if you can't get anything done in more than a decade in office, do you really deserve to be in office in the first place?

## 5. BAN POLITICAL CONTRIBUTIONS WHILE CONGRESS IS IN SESSION

If we were creating a Congress from scratch, is there any way that we would want members of Congress trolling for donations at night while they are trying to legislate during the day?

Put aside the obviously atrocious optics of some political action committee donating a boatload of cash to a senator soon after he votes in favor of its pet bill (quid pro quos are almost impossible to prove legally, but regular people know that sort of thing stinks badly). From a purely logistical perspective, it's almost impossible to juggle the heated policy discussions that go on during congressional sessions with the ever-increasing need to raise the millions of dollars you need to keep your job.

Banning political contributions for House members and senators during the time Congress is in session would make clear that when in Washington, the job of our elected representatives is to craft legislation, not to collect checks. It's not unheard of, particularly at the state legislative level, where lawmakers are often banned from raising any campaign cash during sessions.

Incumbents, particularly those in swing districts, wouldn't like the ban, believing that it would force them to tie one hand behind their back when running against a challenger who was not operating under the same fund-raising constraints. (On a related note: members in safe districts would love this ban, as they would be freed to focus exclusively on legislation rather than on spending time raising money that they almost certainly don't need to win reelection.) But the advantages of incumbency—from broad name identification in a district or state to the ability to raise money from a variety of national sources—more than make up for any disadvantage to members of Congress by a ban on in-session political contributions. Plus, leveling the financial playing field even slightly in favor of challenger candidates would be a good thing, ensuring that more turnover in seats was a real possibility.

In modern politics, the appearance of impropriety is the equivalent of actual impropriety. Voters believe that their elected officials are bought and paid for by moneyed interests who have their own bottom line in mind, not the best interests of the country. While that may not be the reality—members forever insist that political donations don't sway their votes—it really doesn't matter. The only way to win back public confidence, not to mention create space for legislators to, you know, actually legislate, is to ban political contributions during congressional sessions. Given the relatively lax schedule that the House and Senate operate under—who else gets to take the entire month of August off?!—they still should have plenty of time to raise the cash they need to run credible campaigns for reelection.

# CLEAR EYES, FULL HEARTS, RON PAUL

There is no television show more sacred in The Fix household than *Friday Night Lights,* the NBC series that ran for five seasons (too short!), documenting the lives of those who lived in a town in West Texas that revolved around football.

The hub of the show was the relationship between Eric Taylor (Kyle Chandler), the head football coach at fictional West Dillon High School (Go Panthers!), and his wife, Tami (Connie Britton), a guidance counselor at the school. Eric and Tami had the most believable marriage I have ever seen either on TV or in the movies. They bickered. They overreacted. They worried about their teenage daughter, Julie. They wrestled with how to reconcile their career ambitions with their relationship. It felt real. It was real.

(True story: At the 2009 White House Correspondents Dinner—an annual gathering where the world of political journalists invite celebrities as their guests so that we can gawk at them and wonder why we aren't better looking—I spent virtually the entire night stalking (in a non-creepy way) Chandler and Britton. When I eventually found them together, I went all cotton-mouthed as I tried to explain what the show had meant to my wife and me. They were nice—nicer than I would have been if confronted by a stammering nerd in a tux. Eventually, I just asked if I could take their picture together. They obliged. I tweeted it within seconds and it still maintains a treasured home in my iPhoto.)

It wasn't just the Taylors that made the show (although, without them, the show simply wouldn't be the masterpiece it was). There was the troubled but kindhearted high school running back Tim Riggins (Taylor Kitsch). There was Matt Saracen, the nerdy underdog who makes good as a quarterback and takes care of his aging grandmother too. There was Buddy Garrity, a Panther great who ran a successful car dealership in town—when he wasn't scheming about ways to make the team better. There was Jason Street, the quarterback phenom who breaks his neck and is paralyzed in the first episode of the show but goes on to become a successful sports agent.

*FNL*, as its loyalists call it, had it all: tremendous acting, real-life characters, and, yes, just enough football to keep things interesting. (Seriously, if you have never watched it, or never watched it in its entirety, drop this book—or ebook—and go do it. I can't recommend it highly enough.) The idea that the show would be canceled elicited most of the twelve stages of grief in our family: we were in denial ("This must be a typo or something"), then angry ("Those sons of bitches"), then unreasonably optimistic ("They'll bring it back once they see how many people are upset about it going away"), and then, finally, resigned. So upset were we that *Friday Night Lights* was ending that we waited for months to watch the series finale. It sat on our DVR list like a eulogy not yet read, and even after we did, we couldn't bring ourselves to erase it.

The above paragraph reads like a slight—or slightly larger than slight—exaggeration. It's not. Rather it's a reflection of the right-on-the-verge-of-being-creepy-without-going-over devotion that certain television shows create in their viewer.

It's a rare politician who is able to evoke that sort of passion from supporters. And that's what makes Ron Paul, the Texas Republican congressman, so very interesting. Prior to 2008, Paul toiled in almost complete obscurity, holding a central Texas seat on and off for two decades and running a failed bid for the Senate in 1984 and a failed bid for president—as a Libertarian—in 1988. Paul was known, to the extent that he was known at all, for his opposition to any piece of legislation not specifically enumerated in the Constitution, meaning that he opposed virtually everything that Congress voted on. So resolute was Paul in objecting to what Congress did, he earned the nickname "Dr. No."

And that looked like the end of the line for Paul. Until he decided to run for president in 2008 and, in one of the biggest surprises in modern political memory (aka as long as I can remember), emerged as something of a movement candidate.

Out of the blue, Paul's message started to make sense. The country was sick of fighting seemingly endless (and unwinnable) wars in places they couldn't find on a map. Paul's isolationist foreign policy—his allies say it is more like noninterventionist—solved that. The collapse of the financial sector in late 2008 led people to wonder what the hell the masters of the universe were doing with all that money. Paul had been encouraging a healthy skepticism about monetary policy—he wants to end the Federal Reserve—for years. People hated politicians and all of their hedging of uncomfortable truths. Paul seemed to revel in the telling of uncomfortable truths.

It started slowly and, as these things tend to do, out of sight of the mainstream media, who had grown accustomed to dismissing Paul. The first signs were Paul's surprisingly strong fund-raising totals, fueled largely by his success in collecting cash on the Internet. In 2007, Paul raised $2.4 million from April 1 to June 30 and then $5.3 million between July 1 and September 30—unheard-of sums for a candidate who received no national media attention and barely registered in polls on the race.

That something—no one, including Paul, really knew what—was happening was clear. And it was during that time when I had my first experience with the PaulPeople. The moment was the 2007 Ames straw poll, when Paul was regarded as a pleasant sideshow at best and not regarded at all at worst. (Remember, the opposite of love is not hate but indifference.) From the second I stepped out of my car on the campus of Iowa State University, however, the atmosphere felt like nothing I had ever experienced at a political event. Old Volkswagen buses and motorcycles bearing homemade RON PAUL FOR PRESIDENT signs lined the walk into the Ames straw poll. And once you got into the event itself, it felt more like a Phish concert—without the Glow Sticks—than a Republican political event. Groups of Paul supporters danced in conga lines through the Ames site, banging tambourines, drums, and whatever else they could find and chanting "RON PAUL! RON PAUL! RON PAUL!" On the outskirts of the straw poll grounds was a tent packed to the gills with Paul-ites, all waiting for the chance to glimpse their candidate.

The incongruity between the youth and energy of the crowd and Ron Paul is, literally, impossible to quantify in words. Paul has all the look of your grandfather crossed with Montgomery Burns. His stooped stature, too big suit jackets, and relatively soft-spoken nature make him an unlikely rebel or head of a movement. But his ideas—and the clear-eyed belief with which he holds them—had somehow transformed this lifetime backbencher in Congress into just that. And Paul was loving every minute of it.

There was talk among the reporter class as the votes were tallied at Ames that Paul might be the surprise of the day. Talk of a second-place finish behind the incredibly well-organized and well-financed Mitt Romney, the former governor of Massachusetts, was not ruled out. Those predictions—like many predictions made by the professional journalist class (of which I am an unapologetic member) proved grossly misguided. Paul received just 1,305 votes, finishing a distant fifth.

He went on to raise millions more for his campaign—a whopping $28 million by the end of 2007—but was unable to win (or come close to winning) a single primary or caucus in 2008. The conclusion most people drew was that Paul, and the people who wildly supported him, didn't matter, that there had simply been a temporary rip in the "way we know how politics works" fabric that was quickly repaired.

But that misses the point. It wasn't that Paul and his supporters didn't represent something real. They did. They represented the Libertarian wing within the Republican Party, the people in the party who wanted to be left the hell alone by their government and, in turn, leave the rest of the world the hell alone.

The problem for Paul was that there just weren't enough people who thought like him within the Republican Party. No one's support ran deeper than Paul's, but no one's was as narrow either. If you loved Ron Paul, you really, really loved him. Loved him enough to change your middle name to "RonPaul"—this really happened—or to harangue anyone, anywhere on the Internet who dared to write a negative word about him. (Based on personal experience, I can tell you that the Paul-ites are the most organized ferreters-out of negative—or anything close to it—analysis related to their guy.)

It's like me and Mrs. Fix with *Friday Night Lights*. If people I knew bad-mouthed the show or said they didn't watch it, my opinion of them was immediately affected—and not in a good way. For Christmas, birthday, Valentine's Day, and anniversary, I looked for *FNL*-related merchandise to buy Mrs. Fix. I proselytized about the show to anyone who showed even a passing interest in it.

The problem for me and Ron Paul? They're just aren't enough people who think like us out there. Every year there was chatter that *Friday Night Lights* would be canceled because of its less than stellar ratings. (An important aside: after way too much thinking about it, I have concluded that the show was doomed from the start because of a totally wrongheaded marketing campaign to initially introduce it to the American public. It was regarded first and foremost as a football show, which, well, it wasn't. Casting it as a show that revolved around football turned off a lot of people who could have/would have been loyal viewers of a show that, yes, had a football theme but was fundamentally about growing up and growing old in a small town. By the time the show started to win critical acclaim and even awards, it was too late. The collective American attention span had already categorized *FNL* as a sports show. And there was no looking back.) The show held on for five seasons by its fingernails and the actors involved acknowledged they were happy to have lasted that long.

So too Ron Paul's presidential campaign. While in 2012, Paul expanded his universe of dedicated Paul-ites—he got two and a half times as many votes in the 2012 Iowa caucuses as he had four years earlier—it still wasn't anywhere close to a majority (or even a plurality) of Republicans voting in early states. Paul finished third in Iowa, a distant second in New Hampshire, fourth in South Carolina, and fourth in Florida. In Idaho's caucuses, where he had received 24 percent in 2008, he got just 14 percent this time around. Alaska, where Paul's distrust-of-government message seemingly would find fertile soil, handed him a distant third-place finish behind both Romney and former Pennsylvania senator Rick Santorum.

Privately, Paul advisers acknowledged that his limitations—most of which stemmed from his foreign policy views—meant he would never be a majority (or even close to it) candidate for the Republican Party. It was, in fact, his greatest strength and biggest weakness. The people who loved Paul were drawn to his calls to return troops to America and stop acting like the policeman of the world. If Paul backed away from that viewpoint—or hedged it in any way—many of those Paul-ites would have turned their backs on him. Paul's refusal to do so endeared him forever to his fans but simultaneously ensured he would never grow into anything other than a niche candidate.

Ron Paul and *Friday Night Lights* will be remembered similarly by those that loved them. They were too ahead of their time for mass consumption, fundamentally misunderstood by those who could have liked them, and recalled with fierce devotion by those who loved them.

# CHARGING AT POLITICAL WINDMILLS

Every four years, they appear—the candidates running for president who clearly have no chance of actually being elected but who devote months and sometimes even years to tilting at windmills.

The list of quixotic candidates is long and largely undistinguished—filled with might-have-beens like former Connecticut senator Chris Dodd, who ran for the Democratic presidential nomination in 2008, has-beens like former Pennsylvania senator Rick Santorum, who ran for president in 2012, and never-will-bes like Alan Keyes, who ran for president in 1996 and 2008.

Or what about Carol Moseley Braun, who, after losing her Senate race as a Democrat in Illinois—no easy task—decided that making a presidential run in 2004 made all the sense in the world. That view was not widely held by voters, donors, or activists. Braun dropped out of the race just days before the Iowa caucuses and endorsed former Vermont governor Howard Dean, who went on to crash and burn in the Hawkeye State.

Or Alexander Haig, who after a distinguished career of service in the Nixon, Ford, and Reagan administrations—he spent time as White House chief of staff and secretary of state—decided to run for president in his own right in 1988. It seemed a kamikaze mission from the start designed to derail then vice president George H. W. Bush. In a 1987 debate Haig famously told Bush "I never heard a wimp out of you" regarding a nuclear treaty—a put-down that was widely regarded as Haig's attempt to cast Bush as insufficiently tough to be president. Bush laughed last, however. He became the Republican nominee and the president. Haig, on the other hand, dropped out of the race before the New Hampshire primary and endorsed then Kansas senator Bob Dole.

To the average person, it's beyond baffling why these people run. Why spend time, money, and heartache on something where the outcome is not only predetermined but also almost certain to be bad? It's seems odd, at best, and incredibly depressing at worst.

That way of thinking misses the point, however. After all, thousands of people train for marathons—not exactly a joyous thing to put your body through with no expectation of winning the actual race. I play pickup basketball twice a week and do everything I can this side of cheating—and sometimes the other side of cheating—to win, even though the result is ultimately completely meaningless. Winning then need not be the only reason why people take on challenges. In fact, for lots of us it's not a reason at all. The same goes for the men and women who run for president.

Take each of the politicians mentioned above. Each of them is indicative of a major reason why politicians who have no real chance of grabbing the brass ring reach for it anyway.

Let's start with Dodd. On paper, Dodd's résumé was as impressive as anyone's in the 2008 Democratic presidential field. The son of a senator, he spent six years in the U.S. House in the mid-1970s before winning a U.S. Senate seat in 1980. (By the time he ran for president in 2008, Dodd was the longest-serving senator in the long and glorious political history of the Nutmeg State.) He spent two years at the helm of the Democratic National Committee during the 1990s and was seen as a major liberal force—along with his best friend Ted Kennedy—on the policy front in the Senate.

Of course, campaigns aren't fought on paper or in a vacuum. And from the start Dodd was badly overshadowed by bigger names like Clinton, Obama, and John Edwards. Dodd did everything he could to stand out—running ads highlighting his résumé and mane of white hair, moving his family to Iowa for the final two months of the campaign (not kidding, he really did that), and attacking the front-runners as unproven commodities in a dangerous world.

But politics is at least part pizzazz, and Dodd could never find a spark. He looked and felt like the old guy in the race, talking about all the battles he had won in the past rather than about what he would do in the future if he managed to get elected. Despite devoting untold amounts of campaign time to the state—to reiterate, he *moved* his family, including two young daughters, to Iowa in the dead of winter—Dodd failed to get even one percent in the caucuses (gut punch!) and dropped out of the race shortly afterward. To add insult to injury, Dodd's 2008 presidential bid laid the groundwork for his eventual forced retirement from the Senate in 2010, as Connecticut voters didn't love the idea of a guy whose salary they were paying uprooting his family to Iowa for a few months.

So why did Dodd do it? Because he had always wanted to run for president and would have spent his life regretting it if he hadn't given it a try. Remember that Dodd was an up-and-comer on the Democratic political scene for most of the 1980s and early 1990s—he was only thirty-six when he was elected to the Senate—who was always in the mix when conversation turned, as it inevitably always does, to who might run for president at some point down the line.

But the timing just never seemed to work out for him. In 1988, Joe Biden filled the slot of "hotshot young senator" in the presidential race. (Biden was regarded as a major player until a plagiarism scandal. He ripped off lines from a speech given by Neil Kinnock, a Welsh Labour Party politician.) In 1992, Dodd was up for reelection to the Senate, making a presidential run a near impossibility. In 2000, Vice President Al Gore was the heir apparent as the Democratic nominee. Dodd thought seriously about running in 2004 but ultimately decided to bow out and support his home state colleague Joe Lieberman, who had been Gore's running mate four years earlier.

By 2008, Dodd was sixty-four years old—a young upstart gone gray (white, actually) who still carried national ambition inside him. Dodd knew enough about politics to know he had only the longest of long-shot chances to wind up as his party's nominee. But he also knew that he would always wonder what might have been if he didn't run in 2008. And so, he ran. Was it quixotic? His inability to win even one percent in Iowa says that it was. But that doesn't mean it wasn't successful in scratching that itch that had irritated Dodd for the better part of three decades.

Rick Santorum's reasons for running for the Republican nomination in 2012 were, like Dodd's, not centered primarily on winning—although he came remarkably close to doing so. Instead Santorum ran to reclaim his image within the party as a serious and credible person who had a demonstrated appeal to voters—an image that had been severely tarnished when he was destroyed in his bid for a third term by Senator Bob Casey in 2006.

Prior to that eighteen-point defeat, Santorum had put together a mighty impressive political and legislative career. Santorum beat a long-standing Democratic incumbent in a Democratic-leaning western Pennsylvania congressional seat in 1990, and four years later he did it again at the statewide level, ousting then senator Harris Wofford in one of the most high-profile and expensive races of 1994. Despite representing a Democratic-leaning state, Santorum was unabashedly conservative once he got to the Senate—an ideological purity that when coupled with nearly unbridled ambition allowed him to rise through the leadership ranks of the GOP. By 2001, Santorum was the chairman of the Senate Republican Conference, the third-ranking leadership position in the chamber. But his high-profile conservatism in that job sowed the seeds of the defeat that was to come.

Though he had won a second term with ease in 2000 thanks to a lackluster and underfunded Democratic opponent, Santorum was at the top of most target lists heading into 2006. His time in Republican leadership was coupled with a fatigue with President George W. Bush and Republicans more broadly that made 2006 a very difficult year for the party across the country. Santorum's vulnerability was made worse by the candidacy of Casey, the son of the former governor of the state, whose last name remained a major asset in the eyes of voters. From the start of the race, Santorum was doomed; Casey regularly led by double digits in polling and went on to hand Santorum a historically bad defeat for a sitting Senate incumbent.

That defeat turned Santorum into a punch line in the political community, overshadowing all of his previous accomplishments in the process. And so when Santorum made clear that he was planning to run for president in 2012, the overall reaction from the professional political class—Democrats and Republicans—was a collective eye roll. Santorum, of course, knew that and ran to change how history would remember him.

Way back in September 2009 I sat down with Santorum at a coffee shop on Capitol Hill to talk about the prospect of his running for president in 2012. (And, yes, even way back then he was thinking about it.) Here's how he pitched himself: "The beauty that I bring to the table is that I have sixteen years of doing. I have a pretty good record of tapping into the concerns of the American public and effectively following through and passing legislation that has made a difference."

Santorum, even way back then, had his legacy on his mind. He didn't want to be remembered as the guy who lost reelection by eighteen points in 2006. He wanted to be remembered as the guy who ran for president in 2012. And, to his credit, Santorum's hopes of legacy-molding paid off. No one—and I mean no one—thought that Santorum had any chance of winning the Iowa caucuses. He did. No one thought he would have a fighting chance of emerging as the conservative alternative to Mitt Romney. He did.

Santorum ultimately came up short—unable to overcome the financial and organizational advantages enjoyed by Romney. But is there any argument that he emerged from the race as a much bigger—and more respected—figure within the party than he was when he started running? Santorum reclaimed his political life and legacy in his losing bid, which, of course, makes his candidacy the opposite of quixotic.

If Santorum was running to prove something, Alan Keyes ran to say something. Or a lot of things, to be more accurate. Keyes is a prime example of the perennial candidate, a person whose job—whether or not he is willing to acknowledge it—is to run for public office as a way of keeping his name and voice in the public dialogue.

All told, Keyes has run six times unsuccessfully, three times for president and another three (1988 and 1992 in Maryland, 2004 in Illinois) for Senate. (That last race came against Barack Obama; Keyes, who lived in Maryland, was recruited to run by an Illinois Republican Party desperate to field a candidate after it lost its nominee in a sex club scandal. Yes, all of that really happened.)

In each of his races, Keyes focused almost exclusively on the ills of abortion. (Keyes accused the candidate Obama of adopting the "slaveholder's position" by supporting abortion rights during the 2004 Senate race.) While he talked quite a bit—Keyes is an eloquent debater and speaker—he rarely if ever talked about the sort of kitchen table issues in which voters were interested. It's not surprising then that Keyes was a total nonfactor in every one of the races that he ran in. (His best showing ever was 38 percent in his 1988 race against Democratic senator Paul Sarbanes.)

Winning, of course, was entirely besides the point for Keyes. His goal was to give his views on things like abortion and homosexuality as wide an airing as possible. Keyes always ran causes, not campaigns. Without the megaphone afforded to him by running for president, Keyes's viewpoints would have never reached as big an audience as they ultimately did. Running then was a means to an end for Keyes. It allowed him a platform, which he could get no other way, to voice his views. The very fact that he was included in debates that aired on national cable television was a major victory for Keyes.

There's also another, more capitalist reason why people like Keyes run. In raising their profile—"presidential candidate" looks pretty nice on a résumé—they raise their earning power. Keyes's speaking fees likely went through the roof after his 2004 Senate race and 2008 presidential bid. He became a national figure, a hot commodity for conservative groups looking for speakers and for other organizations looking to affiliate with a recognized champion of the conservative movement. His candidacies also help drive attention to—and sales of—his book, *Our Character, Our Future,* which was released in 1996 and can be bought for $3.04 on Amazon at the moment.

The broader point here is that candidates run for office for all sorts of reasons. The main reason is to win, but there is a whole substrate of candidates for whom winning is almost beside the point. Remember that Don Quixote has become a symbol not of hopelessness but of valor in our society. Just because a candidacy is quixotic doesn't mean it's pointless.

# THE FIX ENDORSEMENT HIERARCHY

Political endorsements are a dime a dozen. Every day someone is endorsing someone else's campaign. The endorsee is touting the endorser as a critical piece to the winning electoral puzzle. Headlines are written. News is created.

I wanted something more. There had to be something better. (And, yes, those two sentences kind of sound like the introduction to me founding some sort of new religion.) And I knew from years of covering politics that not all endorsements were created equal; some mattered more, some mattered less, most didn't matter at all. So I set out on a quest to build my own system of ranking endorsements from most to least meaningful.

As my guide—in this and all things—I looked to Bill Simmons (aka the Sports Guy). Simmons is one of the most imaginative and interesting thinkers in journalism these days and has been hugely influential in my approach to what I do. (I've had the pleasure of meeting Simmons once—our conversation was sort of like when Chris Farley interviewed Paul McCartney on *Saturday Night Live;* I'll give you one good guess which one of us played the Farley role.) Simmons thinks differently—and, frankly, better—than most people covering sports. My goal has been, is, and always will be to do the same for politics.

Simmons had long developed and nurtured a feature he called the "Levels of Losing," an attempt to quantify the depths of various kinds of defeats in sports. An example: "Level XV: The Achilles' Heel: this defeat transcends the actual game, because it revealed something larger about your team, a fatal flaw exposed for everyone to see. . . . Flare guns are fired, red flags are raised, doubt seeps into your team. . . . Usually the beginning of the end. (You don't fully comprehend this until you're reflecting back on it.)"

I wanted that. But for political endorsements. And since it didn't exist, I decided to create it. In a scene not that dissimilar from the creation of The Monster in *Young Frankenstein*, I built the Fix Endorsement Hierarchy. (I put all the creativity into the actual hierarchy, leaving almost nothing for the name of the project.) Below is my much-edited, always-being-refined Fix Endorsement Hierarchy. The endorsements are ranked from least desirable to most.

## THE PARIAH ENDORSEMENT

What it is: most endorsements can draw a day's worth of positive headlines for the endorsee. Not so the pariah endorsement, the backing of a politician so damaged that other pols avoid it, well, like the plague.

Best-case scenario: picking a best-case scenario for a pariah endorsement is sort of like being the tallest midget; it's not really much of an accomplishment. If you happen to be on the receiving end of a pariah endorsement, the best you can hope for is that it gets ignored by the media and most voters, and that the pariah endorser stays out of sight for most (or all) of the election.

During the 2008 election, then senator Barack Obama seemed to be enjoying a best-case-scenario pariah endorsement when it came to Reverend Jeremiah Wright. Wright, the controversial pastor of the church Obama and his family had attended, had largely lain low in the campaign. (Obama referred to him in the spring of 2008 as "an old uncle who says things I don't always agree with.") Then in March of that year, ABC News unearthed sermons in which Wright said, among other things, that black people should not sing "God Bless America" but rather "God Damn America" and suggested that the United States bore considerable responsibility for the terrorist attack of September 11, 2001.

Days later, Obama denounced Wright in a much-acclaimed speech about the state of race relations in the country. While Wright caused Obama and his campaign team significant agita during the race, he also became the pivot point for Obama to speak about race and his vision for the country in a way he might not have been able to do without the Wright controversy swirling.

Worst-case scenario: from 1998 until 2008, John Edwards was one of the hottest things in Democratic politics at the national level. His 2004 "two Americas" speech reset the Democratic worldview by suggesting that there was a system of haves and have-nots in the country and his party was the one looking out for all of them. Edwards remained a major figure until October 2007 when the *National Enquirer*—yes, that's who broke the news—ran a report alleging that Edwards had had an affair with a former campaign staffer. Edwards call the report "completely untrue." By August 2008, Edwards admitted he was having an affair with a woman named Rielle Hunter but denied that he had fathered her child. After an elaborate ruse involving a male staffer being paid off to say he was the child's father, Edwards admitted—finally—in January 2010 that he had fathered the child. Did I mention that over that time his wife's cancer had returned? And that the two of them held a press conference announcing it was incurable but that Edwards would run for president in 2008 anyway? And that she passed away in December 2010? So, that happened.

As you might imagine, Edwards went from Mr. Popular to persona non grata during that four-year act of political hari-kari. Edwards is rarely seen in public these days—would you go out if everyone in the world knew that story about you?—but if he ever decided he wanted to dip a toe back into the political waters with an endorsement, you can bet the potential endorsee would reject the idea out of hand. Edwards is a political pariah and the godfather of the pariah endorsement.

## THE NONENDORSEMENT ENDORSEMENT

What it is: Alison Krauss sings a song that goes: "You say it best, when you say nothing at all." The nonendorsement endorsement is just that: a politician refuses to endorse for fear of a boomerang effect that comes back and hurts his/her own career.

Best-case scenario: In 2010, Louisiana Republican senator David Vitter was three years removed from admitting his involvement in the "DC Madam" prostitution scandal. He also happened to be up for reelection to a second term. Even though Vitter's poll numbers were relatively strong and he looked like a pretty good bet to win, Bobby Jindal, Louisiana's very popular Republican governor, simply refused to throw his support to Vitter.

"What continues to be true is we have not yet endorsed in any of the federal races in Louisiana," Jindal said in September 2010 in a classic bit of political speak. Earlier in the month, he was even clearer about his level of ambivalence about Vitter: "Voters in Louisiana are smart enough to make up their own minds and decide who to vote for," said Jindal. Ouch.

Jindal, who has presidential aspirations, just didn't want to be seen—in any way, shape, or form—as having condoned Vitter's extramarital activities, for fear that his support of the senator could be used against him in a national race down the line. Vitter tried to pressure Jindal into an endorsement, but the governor held firm. Vitter went on to win easily, but it's hard to imagine Jindal has any regrets about how things turned out.

Worst-case scenario: Caution is rarely a good thing in American politics. Fortune favors the bold, and you often pay a steeper price for not endorsing than for getting involved.

Witness the 2010 Senate primary between former Florida state representatiave Marco Rubio and Governor Charlie Crist. Crist was a huge favorite in the race, and although many Republican elected officials doubted Crist's conservative credentials and liked Rubio's fresh-faced appeal, they avoided getting involved in the race on Rubio's behalf.

Then Rubio caught fire—turning into a national Tea Party celebrity and a symbol of the rebirth of true conservatism within the GOP. Not surprisingly, politicians—those eyeing bids for president in 2012 and the merely ambitious—fell all over one another to get behind Rubio. He graciously accepted all of the laurels thrown at his feet, but it's hard to imagine he didn't keep a running mental list of who had been with him when times were hard and who was a fair-weather friend. Being late to the Rubio party in 2010 likely means you won't get an early invite when—not if—he runs for president in 2016 or 2020.

## THE "ME FOR ME" ENDORSEMENT

What it is: sometimes endorsements are more about the person giving them than the person receiving them. When I think about the "me for me" endorsement, I always think about a Father's Day in the mid-1980s when I bought my dad an Atari 2600 as a gift. Man, he really wanted that Atari.

Best-case scenario: Former Nebraska Republican senator Chuck Hagel would love to be in the Obama administration. Like, a lot. So when he decided to endorse Pennsylvania Democratic representative Joe Sestak's bid for the Senate in 2010, the motivation was slightly transparent. Hagel—surprise, surprise!—touted Sestak's independence and his military record. (Hagel was heavily decorated during the Vietnam War.)

While Hagel's endorsement might have helped him burnish his I-am-not-tied-too-closely-to-the GOP credentials some, it did nothing for Sestak. While Hagel was a popular figure in Georgetown salons, he was a virtual unknown to the average Pennsylvania voter. Sestak wound up losing the race—but not because of Hagel. (Of course, had Sestak won, it would have had nothing to do with Hagel either.) And Hagel is still waiting on that appointment to a cabinet post in the Obama administration.

Worst-case scenario: Former Utah governor Jon Huntsman endorsed Mitt Romney's presidential campaign when he decided to end his longshot bid for the GOP nod this year. At the time, Huntsman said that "despite our differences" Romney was the best candidate to beat President Obama.

What Huntsman figured was that he might get some boost from the party establishment for getting out quickly after his loss in the New Hampshire primary. And, given the fact that all of the other remaining candidates looked to be longshots, backing Romney almost certainly meant that Huntsman would be with the guy who would wind up as the nominee—and maybe the president. If Romney got to the White House, it followed that Huntsman might well be in consideration for a plum cabinet post.

Even in the moment it didn't feel like Huntsman's heart was really in the endorsement—the Huntsman and Romney families have long been rivals—and the way he has acted since making it proves that he never really meant it. The only time Huntsman has made news in regards to Romney since endorsing him is on the negative side. He criticized Romney's approach to China in an interview with MSNBC and has made no attempt to hide his desire for the emergence of a third party. Huntsman's daughter, Abby, went as far as to tell ABC in April that her dad "is not a surrogate for Romney and will not be out stumping for him in the general." Gee, thanks. Huntsman's "me for me" endorsement won't wind up doing him any good (can you

imagine Romney giving him an administration job now?) and certainly didn't help Romney any.

## THE OBLIGATORY ENDORSEMENT

What it is: lots of times—particularly in presidential races—there is
an expectation that high-ranking officials in the party will endorse
their nominee, no matter how much they hate that person. Hence the
obligatory endorsement.

Best-case scenario: John McCain was very bitter after he came up
short against George W. Bush in the 2000 Republican presidential
primary. And for good reason. McCain had endured any number of
indignities at the hands of the Bush team during the primary process
that year. In South Carolina, rumors were spread that McCain had
fathered a black child out of wedlock; he and his wife had, in fact,
adopted a Bangladeshi girl years before. (That whisper campaign was
never traced back to Bush, and he and his senior strategy team denied
involvement.) So angry was McCain that he condemned "agents of
intolerance" within the party in a much-covered speech at Bob Jones
University in the wake of his South Carolina loss and, even after the
primary ended, made clear his disdain for Bush and the way that
he had won. (One of McCain's top advisers, John Weaver, left the
Republican Party for a time following that 2000 primary in protest for
the way the nomination fight had played out. He eventually returned.)

With such hard feelings from the 2000 race, there was considerable
speculation about how McCain might handle things when Bush was
up for reelection in 2004. McCain quickly put any talk of a lingering
rift to bed with a full-throated endorsement of Bush and a pledge
to work at helping him win a second term. To the surprise of many,
McCain made good on that promise—campaigning anywhere and
everywhere for Bush; he even cut an ad for Bush touting the incumbent's hard-line stance on the war on terror. Bush's narrow 2004 victory might not have been possible without McCain.

(Worth noting: McCain made a best-case obligatory endorsement out of necessity. He was already plotting a second run for president in 2008 by the time Bush stood for a second term and knew that he could never win the Republican nomination with the Bush team actively working against him. It was an act of political survival—and it worked, as McCain went on to be the GOP nominee in 2008.)

Worst-case scenario: McCain had made his career in the Senate as a nonconformist, so it's not all that surprising that as it became more and more clear that he would be the Republican nominee in 2008, there were lots of his colleagues who resisted getting in line behind him. One particularly good example was Thad Cochran, the Mississippi senator and highest-ranking Republican on the powerful Appropriations Committee. That perch put him at daggers drawn with McCain, who has spent a career railing against just the sort of earmarking—designating federal funds for pet projects in your state or district—that Cochran and the broader Appropriations Committee had made a political living on for years.

Cochran endorsed Mitt Romney's 2008 presidential campaign, and in late January 2008 he said that the thought of McCain as president "sends a cold chill down my spine. He is erratic. He is hotheaded. He loses his temper and he worries me." *Damn.* Less than a month later, Cochran endorsed McCain—following Romney's departure from the contest. "I am supporting John McCain for the Republican nomination for president," wrote Cochran in a statement sent to reporters that then went on for three more sentences in praise of, wait for it, Romney. Ladies and gentlemen, the obligatory endorsement!

## THE WHAT-GOES-AROUND-COMES-AROUND ENDORSEMENT

What it is: revenge is, of course, a dish best served cold. And there is no more revenge-laden arena than the political one, where grudges can last for decades.

Best-case scenario: in the 2008 Republican presidential race, for-mer New York City mayor Rudy Giuliani was certain that he had the endorsement of then Florida governor Charlie Crist in his pocket. Knowing he had to have Florida to remain relevant in the presidential race, Giuliani had relentlessly courted the popular Crist for months and, during a Crist visit to the Hamptons in July 2007, became con-vinced that the endorsement was his. Then Crist endorsed Arizona senator John McCain just two days before the Florida vote. With the rug pulled out from under him, Giuliani collapsed in the Sunshine State—a defeat that effectively ended his campaign.

Two years later, he got his revenge though. Crist was now run-ning for the Senate and found himself in a surprisingly competitive primary against a relative political unknown named Marco Rubio. Crist's popularity had taken a major hit by that point, and it was al-ready clear that Rubio was well on his way to pulling the upset. With Crist already down, Giuliani saw his moment to kick the governor square in the balls. And, like a true New Yorker, he did so—with relish. Giuliani endorsed Rubio—despite the fact that Rubio was considerably more conservative than Giuliani—and in a conference call announcing the endorsement noted that Crist had "broken his word" about the 2008 endorsement. Crist eventually dropped out of the Republican primary, switched his party affiliation, and ran unsuccessfully as an independent in 2010. And Giuliani loved every minute of it.

Worst-case scenario: Rick Santorum and Arlen Specter were both Republican senators from Pennsylvania. And that's about where the similarities stopped. But, though they existed on the extremes of the GOP—Santorum on the right, Specter on the left—they forged a mutually beneficial political relationship. Specter helped Santorum appeal to moderate Republicans and independents living in the Philadelphia suburbs during the general election, while Santorum protected Specter's right flank from a serious primary challenge.

Specter got just that in 2004 when conservative representative Pat Toomey challenged him. Specter needed Santorum's stamp of approval to win back wayward conservatives dissatisfied with his moderation on most issues. And he got it. Campaigning with the backing of Santorum and then president George W. Bush, Specter pulled out a squeaker—51 percent to 49 percent.

In the years since the endorsement, a lot has changed—most notably that Specter left the Republican Party for the Democratic side in 2009, a move that gave Democrats a sixty-seat filibuster-proof majority for a time. Specter ran and lost in a Democratic primary in 2010; his seat was eventually won in the general election by Toomey.

Santorum has since said he made a "political decision" to endorse Specter in 2004 and acknowledged that his wife, Karen, was against the move. But those admissions didn't stop his political rivals in the 2012 Republican presidential nomination fight from jumping on him for endorsing one of the most reviled men within the GOP.

Santorum, of course, never wanted to endorse Specter in the first place. Once he did, he got pilloried for it. And Specter is now beyond his reach for revenge—not only a Democrat but also now out of office. Oomph. Actually, double oomph.

## THE NEWSPAPER ENDORSEMENT

What it is: this one is kind of self-explanatory.

Best-case scenario: in the spring of 2009, state senator Creigh Deeds was running for the Democratic gubernatorial nomination in Virginia. He was being overshadowed and outspent by state delegate Brian Moran and former Democratic National Committee chairman Terry McAuliffe. Then the *Washington Post*—disclaimer: I work for them, in case you somehow didn't know—endorsed Deeds, and everything changed. The *Post* editorial page remains an influencer among the northern Virginia smart set, which also happens to be a major bloc of voters in a Democratic primary in the Commonwealth.

The endorsement of Deeds validated him in some important way to those sorts of voters; he went from also-ran to runaway primary winner within the space of a few weeks. In the general election, it was a different story though. The *Post* endorsed Deeds over then state attorney general Bob McDonnell (R), but the Republican cruised to victory anyway.

Worst-case scenario: almost every other newspaper endorsement. Other than the *Washington Post* in the DC Metro area and the *New York Times* in New York City, it's difficult to think of even a handful of newspaper endorsements that have really mattered in politics in recent years. Take the *Des Moines Register* endorsement in the 2008 Democratic presidential primary. Hillary Clinton, Barack Obama, and John Edwards all competed furiously for it, and the media—yours truly included—covered it as though the entire fate of the Iowa caucuses hinged on whom the *Register* picked.

I still remember vividly being at a dinner party with Mrs. Fix on that Saturday night in late December 2007 when the *Register* endorsement was going online. I had come prepared with my laptop and AirCard—what a great dinner guest, right?—and immediately upon arrival sequestered myself in the bedroom, hitting refresh over and over again on the *Register* home page, waiting for their pick to pop up. (It's kind of like trying to get concert tickets except *way* less cool.) The *Register* wound up picking Clinton, an endorsement that was touted by most political observers as a sign of her late momentum in the state. Or not. She wound up finishing third in Iowa, well behind Obama.

## THE CELEBRITY ENDORSEMENT

What it is: an entertainer, author, reality star, or someone else who lives in the world of celebrity decides that the normal world needs to know who they think would make a good candidate.

Best-case scenario: action star—I can't believe I just wrote those two words together—Chuck Norris and former Arkansas governor Mike Huckabee were, weirdly, two peas in a pod. Norris—and the whole "Chuck Norris Facts" Internet meme that had grown up around the man who once played Walker, Texas Ranger—was a perfect fit for the quirky populism of Huckabee. And Norris wasn't simply a sideshow in Huckabee's campaign. In fact, Huck actually ran ads featuring Norris: "My plan to secure the border? Two words: Chuck Norris," said Huckabee in one ad. (I am not kidding, that really happened.) Norris's involvement in the Huckabee campaign reinforced the idea that this was not your father's Republican presidential candidate. And, somehow, it worked. Really, really well.

Worst-case scenario: reality "star" Donald Trump's last-gasp grasp for relevance was to throw his support behind Romney—in Las Vegas no less! Trump, who came to political "prominence" thanks to his fact-less assertion that President Obama might not have been born in the United States, was perhaps the only person who was interested in whom he might support for president. Romney would have been thrilled to never be endorsed by Trump at all but offered a brilliant commentary on the absurdity of it all while standing side by side with Trump. "There are some things that you just can't imagine happening in your life," Mr. Romney said. "This is one of them." It's funny because it's true.

## THE NATIONAL ENDORSEMENT

What it is: a national political figure endorses a candidate running for president or some other down-ballot office.

Best-case scenario: New Jersey governor Chris Christie supporting Romney in 2012. Christie, who became a national conservative hero thanks to a take-no-prisoners rhetorical and legislative style, had considered running himself before backing Romney. By getting behind the former Massachusetts governor just days after saying no to the race, Christie made clear that in his mind it was time for the party to start coalescing behind Romney. Christie's support also gave Romney a powerful, well-known, and well-regarded surrogate who could draw positive headlines for him in early states.

Worst-case scenario: two weeks before then Illinois senator Barack Obama's victory in the South Carolina primary in late January 2008, Massachusetts senator John Kerry decided to wade into the race. Kerry, who had been the party's presidential nominee four years earlier, backed Obama with the clear hope of unifying the party and bringing the primary race to an end. Kerry allies touted his three-million-person-strong e-mail list and standing within the party as evidence that he could push former North Carolina senator John Edwards out of the race and help coalesce the party behind Obama. Not so much. Obama won South Carolina easily, but Kerry's endorsement was quickly forgotten and the race continued on for another *four* months—during which time Senator Hillary Clinton beat Obama in Kerry's home state of Massachusetts.

## THE IN-STATE STATEWIDE ENDORSEMENT

What it is: the endorsement of a major elected official in a state that plays host to a critical early presidential primary.

Best-case scenario: Arizona senator John McCain had won back-to-back victories in New Hampshire and South Carolina in the 2008 Republican presidential nomination fight but faced a stiffer test in Florida. Former Massachusetts governor Mitt Romney was spending heavily to revivify his campaign with a win in the Sunshine State, and former New York City mayor Rudy Giuliani had staked his entire campaign on winning the Florida primary. When Florida governor Charlie Crist threw his support to McCain just forty-eight hours before the state voted, it amounted to a tipping point. McCain won Florida and the nomination.

Worst-case scenario: New Hampshire senator Judd Gregg endorsed then Texas governor George W. Bush in advance of the Granite State primary in 2000. Prior to that race, Gregg was widely regarded as the biggest political player in Republican circles. Not so much after it. McCain smoked Bush by nineteen points in New Hampshire and very nearly toppled the heavy favorite in the fight for the nomination. Gregg swung and missed again in 2008 when he backed former Massachusetts governor Mitt Romney and McCain won. Come to think of it, maybe I should rename the worst-case scenario the "Judd Gregg award."

## THE SYMBOLIC ENDORSEMENT

What it is: an endorsement that says more than just "vote for this guy." It can be a passing of the torch, a healing of an old wound, or a laying on of hands.

Best-case scenario: when Massachusetts senator Ted Kennedy backed then Illinois senator Barack Obama in late January 2008, it drew a straight line between the passion and excitement that he and his brothers once stirred within the party and the feeling Obama had engendered during his still relatively brief time in public life. Kennedy made the comparison explicit in his endorsement, calling Obama a "man with extraordinary gifts of leadership and character" and, as such, a worthy successor to his brother John.

Worst-case scenario: when former vice president and kind-of-almost-sort-of president Al Gore threw his backing behind former Vermont governor Howard Dean at the end of 2003, it was meant to send a signal that the establishment of the party had begun to embrace a candidate who had heretofore run his entire campaign against that very establishment. The problem was that Dean's supporters hated the establishment of the party and saw Gore's endorsement—and Dean's willingness to accept it—as a sellout. Gore's backing wound up undermining rather than strengthening Dean's case as he headed into the Iowa caucuses. Then came his election night pledge to take his campaign to every state and then the White House, a rant punctuated with a sort of primal scream. And the rest is political history.

# JEN CRIDER, THE WOMAN NEXT TO THE WOMAN

No one this side of Hillary Clinton is a more high-profile female politician than Nancy Pelosi, the California Democrat who in 2007 became the first woman to be Speaker of the U.S. House. And yet the woman who has long been Pelosi's political aide-de-camp is one of the least well-known figures in American politics.

"There are a bunch of people who when I got the job in Pelosi's office said 'who?'" remembers Jennifer Crider of the time in early 2003 when she was hired to work for the California Democrat.

Up until that point, Crider had toiled in almost total anonymity—one of thousands of Hill staffers content to spend a few years at the seat of government before moving away to start their "real" lives. "I was not on a leadership path ever in my career," said Crider. "I thought I was going to go into policy and work at a foundation."

After spending a year in Rochester, New York, where she worked at Xerox, Crider had moved down to DC—in the middle of the blizzard of 1996—with few plans and little money. She decided to look for work in an odd way; she wrote down all the members of Congress whose names she had heard before and went door to door, handing out her résumé. She got a bite from the office of California representative Bob Matsui—Crider had gone to school at the University of California–Santa Barbara—as an intern. She moved on to Washington State Democrat Jim McDermott's office, where she worked on special projects—and answered phones. When the press secretary job opened up, Crider went for it and got it. By 2000, she was press secretary for Washington State senator Maria Cantwell, and after two-plus years in that role her work with Pelosi began.

Crider had actually met Pelosi while working for McDermott. He was a member of the House Ethics Committee and, as such, huddled with the party leadership in a strategy session before every meeting of the committee. (In those days the Ethics Committee was investigating Newt Gingrich. Yes, the same Newt Gingrich who more than a decade later won the South Carolina presidential primary in 2012.)

And it was another McDermott connection that ultimately landed her the job in Pelosi's office. Brendan Daly was working as Pelosi's communications director. His twin brother was a reporter for the Associated Press covering the Washington State congressional delegation. He had met Crider while working on stories about McDermott. When Brendan Daly told his twin he was looking for a good deputy, Crider's name came up. The rest is history.

But it's a piece of history that isn't all that well known because although Crider almost certainly knows Pelosi better than anyone else in Congress, she doesn't talk much about their relationship. "I have never done a profile," Crider said proudly. "I turned them all down."

But in talking to Crider—she and I have known one another since her early days with the former Speaker—a picture of Pelosi does emerge. "She understands politics and plays a level of three-dimensional chess that very few people do," said Crider with obvious admiration. That level of political planning is what put Pelosi in charge of the House in 2006 after more than a decade in the minority. Recognizing that the second midterm election of George W. Bush's presidency was almost certain to be a good one for her side—the so-called six-year-itch elections tend to be devastating for the president's party—Pelosi not only raised tens of millions of dollars for the effort but also installed Illinois representative Rahm Emanuel, the most cutthroat, politically savvy member of the Democratic caucus, as the head of the party's campaign committee. The result was a sweeping victory that made Pelosi Speaker and made Emanuel, who went on to serve as President Obama's first chief of staff and is now the mayor of Chicago, an even bigger political legend.

While Pelosi and Emanuel rightly received the lion's share of credit for the victory, Crider's role as Pelosi's political consigliere is often overlooked—and shouldn't be. Pelosi tends toward a nicey-nice approach, at least publicly, that has to be backed up with a hammer in private. Crider is that hammer. She describes herself as Pelosi's "enforcer" and adds: "Part of the reason they got me was I was a pit bull willing to say no to people." Telling members of Congress no is never easy, but it's especially difficult as a staffer. Crider thrives at it because everyone on the Democratic side of the aisle—from the members to the staff—knows that when she speaks, it's the equivalent of Pelosi talking. Cross Crider, cross Pelosi. Most people aren't willing to do either.

The Democrats' victory in 2006 was a huge moment for the party and Pelosi. But her raised profile ensured that she would become a major target of the conservative right as the GOP fought to take back control of the House. Her approval ratings slid as she worked to enact President Obama's first-term legislative goals; Republicans cast her as a far-left, San Francisco liberal (she does represent the city by the Bay) who was grossly out of touch with the concerns of the average person. By the time the 2010 election came around, Pelosi was the

Republicans' favorite bogeyman, er, bogeylady. More than four hundred different ads that ran in the 2010 election targeted Pelosi, trying to link the California Democrat to members of her party seeking office all over the country. Even some Democratic members of Congress ran ads trying to gain some space from Pelosi; Mississippi representative Travis Childers, running in a strongly conservative district, touted the fact that he "voted against Nancy Pelosi's agenda 267 times."

It didn't matter. Democrats that ran with Pelosi lost. Democrats that ran away from her lost too. In 2010, Republicans netted a massive sixty-three seats and, with those gains, retook control of the House. At that point everyone—and I do mean everyone—expected Pelosi to go quietly into that good night. Except Pelosi.

Despite calls for her to step aside from some within her own House caucus, Pelosi ran and won—easily—to claim the title of minority leader. What few understood was that the losses in the Democratic caucus in 2010 had hit moderate and conservative members of the party disproportionately hard, meaning that the caucus had grown smaller but also more liberal in the wake of those defeats. And Pelosi had spent years cultivating those relationships to ensure she had the undying loyalty of the liberal wing of her party.

And so Pelosi was back to where she started when Crider was first hired way back in 2003. Not only that but she had a plan to take back what was lost. "She really taught me the value at the beginning of a debate of having an idea of where you want to end," said Crider. "Making sure each step along the process gets you to your goal. Sometimes the longest path is going to be the one that gets you there."

It's not clear whether Pelosi, and Crider, are pursuing the short or the long path as they seek to regain the House majority for Democrats. The last three elections—2006, 2008, and 2010—have been national wave elections in which one party makes major gains (thirty-plus seats) in the House. And that's something that has never happened before in modern political history.

The wide swings of the electoral pendulum are the result of voters—many of whom identify themselves as independents—who are deeply unhappy with both parties and simply go back and forth between the two in each successive election. Need evidence? In 2006, independent voters went for House Democrats by eighteen points. Four years later, they voted for House Republican candidates by nineteen points. That's a thirty-seven-point swing (I was told there would be no math . . .) that makes clear that independents are willing to give one side two/four years to figure things out, and if they don't, they get tossed out. It may be impossible to hold the House majority for long when voters think like that.

That volatility is what gives Democrats hope that just two years removed from a sixty-plus-seat loss in the House that they can net the twenty-five seats they need to reclaim the majority. The key to pulling off that trick is keeping what House Republicans have done over the past two years at the top of voters' minds while keeping Pelosi—and all the negatives that have been attached to her in recent years—somewhere near the back. Pelosi, ever the pragmatic political operative, seems to understand that she can best serve her party by largely avoiding the limelight. She has traveled the country relentlessly raking in money for the Democratic Congressional Campaign Committee and various candidates over the past eighteen months, but her visits are rarely publicized and local media rarely even know she is coming.

Pelosi's behind-the-scenes drive to take back the majority, her allies argue, is evidence that she has never really cared about herself and that her ultimate goal has always been elevating the party. Fair enough. But if Democrats do manage to win the twenty-five seats they need to get back House control, Pelosi's own personal political history will end on a far more positive note; she will be the woman who led her party back to the political promised land, not the woman who cost her party its majority. "My goal is getting her away from the point where she is a caricature," said Crider. Winning back the House this November would go a long way to doing that.

Whatever happens in November, it's clear that Pelosi and Crider will weather it together—as they always have. Crider likes to tell a story about a conversation she had with Pelosi after just a few months on the job in which the California Democrat sat her down and said: "Being a woman in this business you need to think about what you want your career to look like and let's figure out how to get there together." They're still doing that same thing a decade later.

# THE ART OF AN OCTOBER SURPRISE

From The Fix Political Dictionary: *October surprise*
—a last-minute revelation that has the potential to fundamentally change the course of a political campaign.

Good (read: winning) campaigns account for everything. Every weakness of their opponent—and themselves—is researched within an inch of its life; every ad is tested in focus groups to make sure it achieves its intended result; every voter list is checked and then re-checked so that no votes are left on the table.

But as in life, it's impossible in a campaign to account for every eventuality. And in the past decade or so it seems as if in almost every major election there is a bombshell that comes to light in the final weeks—or even days—that threatens to rewrite the narrative of the campaign. (It doesn't always do so, but more on that later.) The October surprise has become so commonplace that political strategists begin speculating about what it will be—and politicians start fretting what it will be—as soon as Labor Day ends and the campaign officially begins.

Why has the October surprise grown so prevalent in our modern political culture? Because we are people that now expect last-minute twists—everywhere. We like misdirection in our TV shows (*Lost*, anyone?) and our movies (Kevin Spacey *was* Keyser Söze!). We always expect a hidden surprise lurking around the corner, something that will force us to reevaluate everything we thought we knew. And, of course, politics is in the habit of giving people what they want. So now we seem to have not only an October surprise in every election nowadays but also a growing belief that these "surprises" are anything but surprising—that they are, in fact, orchestrated attempts to change the course of elections. Heck, *Wag the Dog* was an entire movie built around the idea that a fictional president started a war in order to create a distraction from his own sex scandal!

The only way to fully understand the art of the October surprise is to trace it back to its origins. And that brings us to the 1972 presidential race between President Richard Nixon and South Dakota senator George McGovern. Nixon, elected in 1968, had spent his first four years grappling with how to bring an end to the Vietnam War that would save face for the United States. By the time 1972 rolled around, the American public had badly soured on the war, and Nixon knew that finding a way out of the conflict was the key to his chances at a second term.

And so when Nixon's secretary of state, Henry Kissinger, declared in a press conference on October 26, 1972, that "peace is at hand" in Vietnam, Democrats cried foul—arguing that the timing of Kissinger's proclamation, which had little to no antecedent, was purely political. It's virtually impossible to prove that claim right or wrong, since Kissinger isn't likely to own up to his motives either way. And there are powerful arguments to be made on both sides of the debate.

Supporting the Democratic point of view is the fact that peace was not, in fact, at hand. After Nixon was reelected, the United States unleashed a series of bombing strikes against North Vietnam. Our military involvement in the conflict didn't end until August 1973 with the Paris Peace Accords. Despite the fact that Nixon told his chief of staff, Bob Haldeman, that he "wouldn't have said" what Kissinger had, he nonetheless went out on the road campaigning on the idea that the conflict was drawing to a close. "As all of you have read or heard on your television tonight, there has been a significant break-through in the negotiations with regard to Vietnam," Nixon said during a campaign event in West Virginia that night. And Haldeman wrote in his diary—what chief of staff keeps a diary anymore?—that the Kissinger announcement "takes the corruption stuff [Watergate] off the front pages, totally wipes out any other news."

The argument against the idea of Kissinger's "peace is at hand" statement as a strategic political gambit is that Nixon's reelection was not in doubt by the time his secretary of state delivered that ultimately erroneous declaration. McGovern's candidacy, which was heavily premised on the idea of ending the U.S. involvement in Vietnam, had never caught fire. Any momentum he had hoped to garner after an extended—and nasty—primary fight was ended when his vice presidential pick, Missouri senator Tom Eagleton, was forced to drop from the ticket after revelations that he had undergone electroshock therapy to deal with depression issues. Nixon had also already successfully cast McGovern's call for an immediate end to America's involvement in Vietnam as erratic and irresponsible. Kissinger's proclamation of peace turned what was a sure win for Nixon into a full-out rout. Nixon won more than 60 percent of the popular vote and 520 electoral votes—one of the most sweeping victories in modern American politics. The Kissinger declaration then was the icing on a cake that was already baked.

Regardless of whether Nixon and Kissinger purposely coordinated the "peace is at hand" press conference or not, the legend of the October surprise was born. And, eight years later, that legend grew, even though the actual surprise never came.

In the days leading up to the 1980 election between President Jimmy Carter and former California governor Ronald Reagan, the country's attention was centered on the Iranian hostage crisis. A year earlier the U.S. embassy in Tehran had been overrun and more than ninety Americans had been taken captive; Carter had spent the better part of 1980 imposing sanctions on the country and negotiating for the release of the hostages. Republicans speculated privately that Carter was waiting until the final days before the 1980 election to announce that a deal had been reached, a moment that would have almost certainly saved what to that point was a badly faltering campaign.

But the deal came too late for Carter as he lost to Reagan and suffered an even greater political indignity when Iran agreed to release the fifty-two remaining hostages on the day Reagan was inaugurated in 1981. That fortuitous timing for the Gipper led Democrats to gripe that Reagan may well have cut a deal with the Iranians to hold off on agreeing to the hostage deal until the election was already decided.

Despite the hubbub surrounding the October surprise that wasn't, the phenomenon disappeared for the next twenty years or so. Neither 1984 nor 1988 had any memorable last-minute revelations. In 1992, some people believed the one-count indictment against Reagan administration secretary of defense Caspar Weinberger for his involvement in the Iran-Contra affair qualified as an October surprise of sorts. It was announced four days before the election, and the charge was dropped before the end of 1992. While it may well have slowed Republican momentum in the race, it's hard to say that the Weinberger news flipped the contest to Bill Clinton.

Six years later, Republicans accused President Clinton of engineering an October surprise in the 1998 midterm elections when he ordered bombings in Sudan and Afghanistan even as he battled allegations about his relationship with White House intern Monica Lewinsky. At the time, Indiana Republican senator Dan Coats said that Clinton "has been consumed with matters regarding his personal life," adding that "it raises questions about whether or not he had the time to devote to this issue, or give the kind of judgment that needed to be given to this issue to call for military action." Comparisons to *Wag the Dog* were everywhere. But the after-action analysis suggested that Clinton was justified in authorizing the strikes—intelligence reports suggested that the strikes could have killed Osama bin Laden and some of his top deputies. The election itself was a wash; Democrats won five House seats, and there was no net gain or loss in the Senate. That virtual tie was a victory for Democrats, particularly in the House, because then Speaker Newt Gingrich had been predicting double-digit gains for his side in the run-up to the election. The results led to his resignation of the speakership—and his resignation from Congress shortly afterward.

The golden age of October surprise elections really began in earnest in 2000 in the presidential race between then Texas governor George W. Bush and Vice President Al Gore. Bush had taken control of a very tight race as summer turned to fall, and most polling conducted in the final weeks of the race showed him with a five- to six-point edge over Gore.

With five days before the election, news came out of Maine that shocked the political world. In 1976, Bush had been arrested for driving under the influence after a night out with, among others, tennis pro John Newcombe. Bush had previously acknowledged that he had struggled with drinking during his thirties but had never gone public with the fact that he had been arrested as a result of it. Bush quickly admitted that the report was true, saying: "I occasionally drank too much and I did that night." He added that the timing of the revelation was "interesting."

The next five days were filled with coverage of the arrest and speculation about how it might impact the race. What we know: Bush's five-point polling edge evaporated. He lost the national popular vote but won the presidency after more than a month of recount drama in Florida. What we don't: how much did the DUI revelation hurt Bush?

Karl Rove, Bush's chief political strategist during the 2000 campaign, believes that the drunk-driving arrest had a profound impact on the race. As he wrote in his 2010 memoir *Courage and Consequence*:

> Did this last-minute revelation of Bush's decades-old DUI hurt? Yes, a lot. First, it knocked us off message at a critical time. . . . Second, we had made a big issue of Gore's credibility and now we had a problem with Bush's. . . . [A] number of people who supported Bush flipped and went for Gore. Second, a larger number of voters—especially evangelicals and social conservatives—decided not to vote, taking votes away from Bush. . . . Before the news broke, we were up in Maine . . . Bush went on to lose Maine. . . . If Bush did drop 2 percent nationally in the vote because of the DUI revelation, then it probably cost him four additional states that he lost by less than 1 percent—New Mexico, Iowa, Wisconsin, and Oregon. Had he won them, . . . [it] would have allowed him to win the White House without Florida. . . . Of the things I would redo in the 2000 election, making a timely announcement about Bush's DUI would top the list.

Whatever you believe about the 2000 election and Bush's DUI, it very clearly ushered in an age in which October surprises were the rule, not the exception. Take 2004, when Bush was standing for reelection amid falling poll numbers and a rapidly eroding belief about the rightness of the war in Iraq.

Bush had premised the entirety of his 2004 campaign on his superior ability to keep the country safe from another terrorist attack. And so Democrats saw conspiracy when, on October 30, 2004, bin Laden released a videotape—his first in three years—threatening another strike on America. While both Bush and Massachusetts senator John Kerry, the Democratic presidential nominee, condemned the release of the tape, it clearly refocused voters on the war on terror and its stakes—a development that most neutral analysts believe aided Bush. Kerry, for his part, is convinced the bin Laden tape cost him the election. "It changed the entire dynamic of the last five days," Kerry told the Associated Press in 2008. "We saw it in the polling. There was no other intervening event. We saw the polls freeze and then we saw them drop a point . . . it agitated people over 9/11."

Given the narrowness of the eventual outcome—Bush carried Ohio by 100,000 votes and with it won a second term—even the slightest impact from the bin Laden video could well have been decisive. (It's also worth noting that Homeland Security Chief Tom Ridge wrote in a memoir of his time in the job that he came under pressure from other senior members of the Bush administration to raise the nation's terror-alert level in the days leading up to the 2004 election: "We certainly didn't believe the tape alone warranted action, and we weren't seeing any additional intelligence that justified it. In fact, we were incredulous. I wondered, 'Is this about security or politics?'" Ridge wrote in his book entitled *The Test of Our Times*.)

Two years later there was another election—and another October surprise. This one came in the form of revelations that Florida Republican representative Mark Foley had sent sexually explicit messages to male members of the House page program. The news broke in late September—so, actually not technically an October surprise—as Congress was preparing to leave for an extended fall recess in advance of the November election.

Although Foley resigned his office on September 30, the scandal—and allegations about how much Republican leaders knew and when they knew it—carried on through much of October, dominating headlines despite GOP officials' best efforts to move on. (There was also considerable back and forth about whether Democrats had held on to the leak of the Foley information until the last possible moment in order to maximize its impact on the election.)

That the result of the election—Democrats regained the House majority after picking up more than thirty seats—was laid at Foley's feet in the after-action analysis is not entirely fair. Republicans were already laboring badly under the six-year-itch phenomenon and deepening dissatisfaction with the direction of the war in Iraq. The Foley scandal further soured voters and, in particular, independents, who voted for Democrats by eighteen points. But the lion's share of blame for what happened to Republicans at the ballot box in 2006 rightly sits at the feet of George W. Bush, not Mark Foley.

When the 2008 campaign came along and with it the candidacy of Barack Obama, who was running to be the first African American president in history, the debate was over what the October surprise would be, not whether there would be one. In fact, the idea of whether Obama was ready to deal with an October surprise became an argument put forward by the presidential campaign of Hillary Clinton during their extended battle for the Democratic nomination. Not only did Clinton's campaign run the now famous "3 AM ad" that was aimed at raising questions about Obama's readiness for some sort of unexpected national security disaster, but Harold Ickes, a top Clinton lieutenant, addressed the idea head-on in a May interview with *Time*'s Mark Halperin. "We don't know enough about Senator Obama yet," said Ickes. "We don't need an October surprise. And [the chance of] an October surprise with Hillary is remote."

Democratic primary voters didn't buy it. But as October approached, speculation ran rampant. What the surprise would be ran the gamut from a book by controversial pastor Reverend Jeremiah Wright, who Obama had distanced himself from earlier in the campaign, to the release of another tape by bin Laden or even another attempted terrorist attack. It turns out that the October surprise we were all waiting for never arrived. In fact, the moment that turned the election had actually happened on September 15, when Arizona senator John McCain oddly declared that the "fundamentals of the economy are strong" at an event in Jacksonville, Florida. Those six words—coming as they did amid as large a financial crisis as the country had seen in decades—painted the Republican nominee as out of touch on the issue that came to dominate the election. As much as Republicans hoped for a last-minute development that might change the course of an election that was shaping up as a sure loss for their side, none came, and Obama cruised to a victory.

When scanning back across the last thirty years of October surprises, there's no question the pace of them has picked up in the last decade or so. What's tougher to know is just how much power things like the Bush DUI in 2000 or the bin Laden tape in 2004 actually had on outcomes. Of course Kerry blames the bin Laden tape for his loss, but it's just as easy to say that his "I voted for it before I voted against it" comments about funding for the war in Afghanistan doomed his candidacy. As for the 2000 race, it could well have been Democrats' superior turnout operation that (nearly) turned the tide for Gore. Getting into the mind of even one voter—much less the collective thought process of a nation—is incredibly difficult to do. Voters choose their candidates, typically, based on a variety of factors—both those they are consciously aware of and those they aren't. These October surprises seem certain to be one of those many factors for lots and lots of people. But October surprises rarely decide elections on their own. So even as they have gotten to be more and more commonplace, the actual impact of October surprises seems to have lessened considerably.

So when this year's October surprise hits, don't act shocked. You knew it was coming. But impress your friends and, more importantly, vanquish your enemies by reminding them that October surprises are (a) not all that surprising, and (b) not as meaningful as everyone assumes. You can thank me later.

And while we're at it, how about a little bit of handicapping of the potential for October surprises this October!

4–1: A report suggests that Iran is closer than we thought to acquiring a nuclear weapon.

10–1: A former member of Romney's Mormon temple comes forward with a tell-all about how his/her experiences with both the religion and Romney raise questions about the governor's fitness for office.

15–1: Investigations into why the federal government funded Solyndra, a failed energy company, produce incontrovertible evidence that the Obama administration's decision was swayed by its relationships with big Democratic donors.

30–1: A book from a former senior official in the Obama administration is released, painting the president as either (a) a dithering weakling or (b) an arrogant jerk unwilling to listen to his advisers.

50–1: Europe's economic problems rear their head again, raising questions about the viability of the world economy.

250–1: A major hurricane threatens Florida and the entire East Coast. (Hurricane season runs all the way through November 30.)

1,000–1: Three words: Reverend Jeremiah Wright. Again.

10 million–1: Evidence is found that shows President Obama's birth certificate may, in fact, have been a forgery.

# THE DOS AND DON'TS OF SURVIVING A POLITICAL SEX SCANDAL

When the history of political sex scandals is written, historians will look back on the past fifteen years as the glory days. Beginning with Bill Clinton's "I did not have sexual relations with that woman, Miss Lewinsky" and ending with Anthony Weiner sending pictures of his wiener—the irony!—to random people on Twitter, this has been the equivalent of the juiced-ball era in Major League Baseball. Every time you think a politician has behaved as badly as possible, someone else comes along and raises (lowers?) the bar even more. It's a pretty amazing run when a governor lying about hiking the Appalachian Trail in order to fly to Argentina to spend time with his "soul mate" isn't the best/worst political sex scandal of the past five years. (We have to give the "best" award to Weiner. I mean, he accidentally tweeted a picture of his junk to all of his Twitter followers, said he had been hacked, then admitted he had done it. Also, his wife was pregnant with the couple's first child at the time. *GUT PUNCH.*)

Having spent so much time covering all of these scandals so close up—that's kind of a gross image—I fashion myself something of an expert on the best way for politicians to handle their very own sex scandals. And let's be honest, there are going to be more of them. Here are my dos and don'ts.

## DO: ADMIT YOU DID IT—IMMEDIATELY

One lesson I've learned from watching tens of thousands of police procedurals on television over the last few years: the cover-up is always worse than the crime. Always.

Politicians, by their very nature, seem to have an extraordinarily strong belief that they can talk their way out of any corner. But in the Internet age, escape is almost never an option, thanks to the electronic trail you leave behind.

Take Weiner. In the moments after sending a tweet out to the world of his meat and two veg, he tried to blame it on a computer glitch. Weiner insisted he would be hiring an electronic security firm to investigate the hacking, but it soon became apparent that Weiner was not a victim but rather a repeat offender. Nine days after he sent the picture, Weiner held a press conference and acknowledged his culpability.

Now, Weiner might have been forced to resign—as he was—whether he immediately admitted to sending the lewd picture or not. But by dragging out the story for more than a week before admitting he had done it, he effectively ended any debate about whether he could survive politically. Sex scandals are like boils; the sooner they are lanced, the better.

# DON'T: DO A PRESS CONFERENCE

Politicians are drawn to the media like a moth to a flame. They know that the press probably isn't good for them, but they can't quit us. That goes triple for a politician trying to survive a sex scandal.

It might seem like a good idea to "clear the air" and let the media ask questions until they run out of questions to ask. It's not. The reality is that for a politician—or any person for that matter—dealing with a major problem in their personal life, it makes no sense that you take your raw emotions public.

There's no better example of why a press conference is *such* a bad idea than Mark "Appalachian Trail" Sanford, the former South Carolina governor and onetime potential 2012 presidential candidate, who spent five days outside of the state (and the country) visiting his mistress in Argentina. When he arrived back in South Carolina, reporters were waiting for him at the airport. Sensing that the situation had already grown desperately out of control, Sanford called a press conference to explain himself. What followed was one of the most compelling—in an awkward way—performances ever by a politician. Sanford, clearly still reeling from watching his entire life implode in the space of ninety-six hours, dedicated the first five minutes or so of the presser to a retelling of how he loved the Appalachian Trail as a kid and how "one desperately needs a break from the bubble, wherein every word, every moment is recorded—just to completely break." (Hello unfortunate word choice!) It only went downhill from there as Sanford bounced between nonsensical statements ("And the biggest self of self is, indeed, self," for example) and incredibly candid acknowledgments that he still felt something for the woman in Argentina who was not his wife. "I spent the last five days, and I was crying in Argentina so I could repeat it when I came back here, in saying, you know, while, indeed, from a heart level, there was something real," said Sanford. Ouch.

Sanford's political career died that day. He had what amounted to a midlife crisis with every camera and every political reporter in the country watching. A written statement released to reporters admitting the affair and apologizing would have at least given Sanford a chance—albeit an incredibly slim one—to remain a relevant force in South Carolina politics. He blew that opportunity the second he stepped up to the mics on that fateful June day.

## DO: REFUSE TO RESIGN

A political sex scandal is the equivalent of a huge wave crashing on your life. For days or even weeks, you are tumbling below the surface with no idea which way is up. Panic starts to seize you as the prospect of it all being over before you are ready to say good-bye becomes more and more real.

How do you survive? Do what surfers do: wait. Don't panic. The wave and its aftermath will pass. The path to the surface will present itself. (Everything I needed to learn about politics, I learned from watching *Point Break*.) Too many politicians make decisions while they are still rolling and tumbling after being hit by the wave. They resign in hopes of getting out of the limelight and avoiding the painful questions they know are coming for them.

But stepping aside right away ignores a basic reality of politics (and human nature): the American public has an incredibly short memory. What seems like a huge deal today might not seem to be such a big deal a few months down the road. And, if it does, you can resign then.

The classic case here is Louisiana senator David Vitter, who acknowledged in 2007—with his wife at his side (more on that soon)—that he had been involved in the "DC Madam" prostitution case. (He called it a "serious sin" but never elaborated.) Calls for Vitter's resignation were immediate and everywhere. He resisted the initial push to step down but was declared dead politically by the press—me included. After all, Vitter had run and won in no small part on his social conservative credentials—as a defender of traditional marriage and all that good stuff. Involvement in a prostitution ring seemed to be the height of hypocrisy and just the sort of thing that voters hate.

Or not. By the time Vitter was up for reelection in 2010, his poll numbers had recovered considerably from the hit they took in 2007, and despite Democrats' best attempts to find a top-tier challenger for him, they failed. While Vitter failed to convince lots of Republican uppity-ups that he was fully rehabilitated—Louisiana governor Bobby Jindal refused to endorse him, for example—it didn't matter, as the incumbent coasted to a second term. In fact, he won with 57 percent of the vote . . . three points higher than he scored when he claimed a first Senate term back in 2004.

There are obvious downsides to this "batten down the hatches" approach—most notably that your wife and kids (if you have them) are forced to muddle through weeks or even months of uncomfortable questions from the media, not to mention the stares and whispers directed their way at malls, grocery stores, and the like. But, politicians are—let's just be honest—most concerned with themselves and their own careers, particularly those who have already stepped outside their marriage and then admitted it publicly. So how this episode affects their wife and kids may not actually be at the forefront—or anywhere close to the forefront—of their minds.

## DON'T: HAVE YOUR WIFE WITH YOU

The key to surviving a political sex scandal is taking the full brunt of the hit on your own. Having your wife by your side when you admit an affair is the opposite of that.

Politicians and their advisers assume—wrongly—that if your wife is with you voters will see it as evidence that she has forgiven you and take that as their cue to do the same. Not so much. Women—and Mrs. Fix is right at the front of this pack—*H-A-T-E* the idea of a woman who has just been cheated on standing next to her philandering husband as he tries to save his political career. And, if women hate you, it's going to be hard for you to survive the immediate aftermath of the scandal.

Eliot Spitzer, the former governor of New York, is our guinea pig to prove this point. Spitzer, famously/infamously, had a habit of paying for sex—by check!—at the Mayflower Hotel when he came down to visit DC. After a federal wiretap implicated Spitzer, he called a press conference—a no-no, as we detail above—two days later to resign his office. At his side was his wife, Silda—and it was there that Spitzer started his remarks. "In the past few days, I've begun to atone for my private failings with my wife Silda, my children, and my entire family," he said. "The remorse I feel will always be with me. Words cannot describe how grateful I am for the love and compassion they have shown me."

Silda Spitzer looked absolutely stricken, as though she knew she was being used as a prop to begin the repair work on her husband's shattered public image but was incapable of doing anything about it. In the days following Spitzer's resignation, it was Silda who became the story. Some prominent women sympathized with her plight—noting that her presence on the stage was a sign that she believed in the vows she had taken on her wedding day, even if her husband had broken them. Others were less charitable: "Stoicism at the skunk's side is overrated," wrote *New York Times* columnist Maureen Dowd.

It seemed that scorned wives—and the husbands who had done the scorning—were listening. When Sanford called it quits, his wife, Jenny, was nowhere to be seen. (The couple have since divorced.) Ditto the wives of New York representatives Chris Lee and Eric Massa—who resigned in 2011 and 2010, respectively. And Anthony Weiner took the podium alone—amid brutal catcalls about the relative size of his member—when he finally stepped down. (Weiner's wife, Huma Abedin, is a longtime aide to Hillary Clinton who knows a little something about dealing with a politician husband's sexual dalliances.)

# DO: AVOID RIDICULOUS EXCUSES

People and especially politicians can justify almost any kind of behavior. But just because you can find a reason why this whole sex scandal is just a simple misunderstanding doesn't mean that anyone really believes it. In fact, you just wind up looking totally ridiculous and even more guilty.

Remember Larry Craig, the Idaho Republican senator who was arrested in a Minneapolis airport on a charge that he was soliciting sex in a men's bathroom? Craig blamed the whole thing on the fact that he uses a "wide stance"—best ever—when relieving himself. (Craig was accused of nudging a man's foot in a separate stall, a common signal that there is an interest in an anonymous sexual encounter.) Amid calls for his resignation, Craig held a press conference—with his wife, wearing sunglasses, by his side—in which he insisted: "I am not gay. I never have been gay." While he managed to hold on to his office until the end of his term, he had by that time become something of a national punch line.

And, speaking of national punch lines, who could forget the saga of New York Democratic representative Eric Massa. In the spring of 2010 news reports suggested that Massa was under investigation by the House Ethics Committee for allegations that he had sexually harassed a male staffer. Massa, trying to defuse the controversy, released a statement in which he acknowledged, "I did in fact use language in the privacy of my own home and in my inner office that, after twenty-four years in the navy, might make a chief petty officer feel uncomfortable." It just got worse from there. Much worse. At a 2009 wedding for another staffer, Massa admitted that after drinking "fifteen gin and tonics and goodness only knows how many bottles of champagne" he had told a male staff member that "what I really ought to be doing is fracking you." Massa also recounted how during his time in the navy he had walked in on a bunkmate masturbating, "smacked him on the leg and said, 'You need any help with that, let me know.' " Just in case you didn't get the idea, Massa added: "You literally can't move two people in that room . . . without getting into each other's knickers." Massa seemed to think his maritime metaphors made sense and explained what he continually tried to dismiss as a series of misunderstandings. Not so much. He eventually resigned his office under heavy pressure from his own party, which recognized that his ship had already sailed. (See what I did there?)

## DON'T: PAY HUSH MONEY

Trying to buy off your mistress and her family (if she has one) makes things worse, not better. From a practical point of view, it provides another way to trace your connection to her. From a legal point of view, it can skirt or outright break campaign finance laws if you try to buy her silence.

Nevada Republican senator John Ensign learned that lesson the hard way—ahem—when it was revealed not only that he had had an affair with a former staffer on his campaign (whose husband was his chief of staff!) but also that his parents had paid the woman and her family off to keep quiet. In April 2008, Ensign's parents shipped $96,000 to the family of Cynthia Hampton, their son's mistress. Ensign said the payments came "out of concern of the well-being for the longtime family friends during a difficult time," but the fact that the money was sent as Cynthia and her husband, Doug, were breaking professional ties with Ensign's office seemed more than a little fishy. That stink grows even stronger when you remember that Ensign resigned his office just one day before he was scheduled to testify in front of the Senate Ethics Committee regarding the potential impropriety of those payments.

A few years before, another former senator with national aspirations named John Edwards trod similar ground. Edwards, as later came to light, was having an affair with a woman named Rielle Hunter, who was shooting short documentary films about his 2008 run for president. Two major donors to Edwards's campaigns—Fred Barron and Bunny Mellon—funneled hundreds of thousands of dollars to Hunter in an effort to keep the affair quiet. Although Edwards has copped to all of that, a trial was under way at the time of this writing as to whether he used any campaign funds as hush money, charges that, if he is found guilty, would carry a hefty fine—upwards of a million dollars—and a potential prison sentence. Edwards has admitted that he solicited the payments to Hunter from Baron and Mellon but has insisted that those funds were personal gifts among friends, not campaign contributions.

# WHY REPUBLICANS ARE HEADED FOR ELECTORAL OBLIVION

(and How They Can Save Themselves)

Republicans have a real chance at winning both the White House and the Senate in November, victories that if they can also hang on to control of the House would give them unfettered control of all three levers of the federal government for the first time since 2004.

If the GOP can pull off that feat in the fall, expect lots and lots to be written about how the country has been and always will be a center-right one where, if Republicans simply play their political cards right, they will be a permanent majority party. But a look at demographic and electoral trends over the past two decades suggests that Republicans are more likely headed to permanent minority status unless they find a way to address their growing problems with the Hispanic community.

The population growth among Latinos is *the* demographic story of the past decade. Between 2000 and 2010, the country's Hispanic population grew by 15.2 million people, more than half of all population growth (27.3 million) in the United States, according to the U.S. Census Bureau. The Hispanic population grew by 43 percent, more than four times as fast as the population as a whole. (Latinos are now 16 percent of the overall population in the country.)

That growth was not limited to a specific region of the country, and, in fact, it was the South and Midwest—two areas not traditionally considered a hotbed for Hispanics—where Latino population increased the most over the past decade. (The Hispanic population grew in the South by 57 percent and in the Midwest by 49 percent.) While more than half of the country's Hispanics still live in three states—California, Florida, and Texas—there were eight states (Alabama, Arkansas, Kentucky, Maryland, Mississippi, North Carolina, South Carolina, and Tennessee) in which the Hispanic population doubled between 2000 and 2010. Hispanic population increased in every single state as well as the District of Columbia over the past decade.

Those growth statistics make clear that the Hispanic community will soon be—if it's not already—the single most coveted voting bloc in the country by politicians of both parties. And that's a very large problem for Republicans. To understand why, you need to look back first before looking ahead. If you go all the way back to 1992, you quickly see that Republicans have been losing the Hispanic vote at the presidential level by overwhelming margins. Bill Clinton carried Hispanics by thirty-six points over President George H. W. Bush and won the group by fifty-one (!) points over Bob Dole four years later. George W. Bush made a concerted effort to court the Hispanic community both in Texas and at the national level; Al Gore beat him among Hispanics by twenty-seven points in 2000, but Bush did narrow his losing margin among Latinos to just thirteen points in 2004. The 2008 election, however, was a return to form as Barack Obama won the Hispanic vote by thirty-six points over Arizona senator John McCain. In 2010, Hispanics went for House Democratic candidates by twenty-two points over House Republican candidates.

Losing the fastest-growing community in the country by somewhere between twenty-five and thirty points in each election is simply not a sustainable model for future electoral success, particularly as Latinos begin to age—it is a remarkably young population—and more and more of them become eligible and registered to vote. And that movement is already happening. In 2004 there were 16.1 million Hispanics eligible to vote; four years later there were 19.5 million, an increase of more than 20 percent in the space of just one presidential election. And in every election since 1992, Hispanics have cast an ever-increasing percentage of the overall vote. In 1992, Hispanics accounted for just 3.8 percent of all votes, but by 1996 that number had risen to 4.7 percent. In 2000, Hispanics were 5.4 percent of all voters, and that number shot up to 6 percent in 2004 and all the way to 7.4 percent in 2008. The trend line for white voters during that same period was headed in the opposite direction; in 1992 white voters were responsible for 85 percent of all votes cast, but that number had dipped to just 76 percent by 2008.

Given the stark reality of the rapid growth in the Hispanic community and the Republican Party's past difficulties in capturing any significant portion of the Latino vote, you would expect the party's candidates for president to be pushing for policies that can attract Hispanics to their cause. And you'd be wrong. During the primary season, the candidates by and large took a hard line on immigration, which is, without question, the dominant issue for most Hispanic voters.

Mitt Romney, the Republican nominee, advocated "self-deportation" for illegal immigrants during the primary season, which, according to the former Massachusetts governor, is "when people decide that they can do better by going home because they can't find work here."

Both Newt Gingrich and Texas governor Rick Perry were pilloried for even the slightest willingness to acknowledge that rounding up the eleven million (or so) people in the United States illegally might not be feasible or humane. (Perry called those who opposed offering in-state college tuition to the children of illegal immigrants "heart-less" during a presidential debate in the fall of 2011; he later apolo-gized for using that language.)

The simple reality is that the conservative base of the Republican party (aka the people who tend to decide the identity of the party's presidential nominee) are vehemently opposed to the idea of any sort of comprehensive immigration reform that creates a path to citizen-ship for anyone who entered the country illegally. Look at the political journey of Arizona senator John McCain for evidence of the perils of crossing the base on the issue. McCain was a major advocate for some sort of comprehensive overhaul of the immigration system in 2007. He walked away from that position as it became clear that it was oblit-erating his chances of being the Republican presidential nominee in 2008. And then in 2010, when faced with a challenge from his ideo-logical right in a Senate primary, McCain seemed to take on the same absolutist position he had rejected less than three years before. In one ad that ran in the primary campaign, McCain is shown walking with a border agent and insisting that we need to "build the danged fence" to cut down on illegal immigration. McCain won that race easily and now has moved back to his previous centrist position on immigration reform. He criticized Romney's "self-deportation" plan and added that "it has to be a very humane approach to this issue, and we have to come up with solutions to it" during an interview with Univision in early February 2012.

McCain isn't the only powerful voice within the party making the case for a fresh start for Republicans with the Hispanic community. Former Florida governor Jeb Bush has been the most high-profile figure calling for a dialing-back of the rhetoric within the party on immigration, going as far as to warn the candidates prior to January's Florida presidential primary that heated talk about illegals was doing their side no good. Bush also penned an op-ed in the *Washington Post* in January laying out the stakes for his party when it comes to the Latino vote. "In the 15 states that are likely to decide who controls the White House and the Senate in 2013, Hispanic voters will represent the margin of victory," wrote Bush. "Just eight years after the party's successful effort to woo Hispanic voters in 2004, this community— the fastest-growing group in the United States, according to census data—has drifted away." Bush outlined in the piece a handful of solutions for solving the Republican immigration problem—focus on the economics of immigration, treat the Hispanic community not as a bloc but as a series of diverse electorates, push education reform to help their children in failing schools, all of which are good ideas.

The problem is that Jeb Bush isn't running for president in 2012, no matter how hard some Republicans tried to get him to consider doing so. And that makes it very easy for Bush to offer solutions without suffering the electoral wrath of a political base that doesn't want to start a serious conversation about immigration policy in the country before all eleven million people who are here illegally are sent home. It's easy to stand on the sidelines and suggest how the players on the field should act. It's much more difficult to be in the middle of a fight for your political life and take the sort of principled stand that you know won't be popular within your own party and might, in fact, cost you the brass ring that you have spent your entire life chasing. (I equate what Bush is doing to those guys who are waiting on the sidelines to play in a pickup basketball game and inject themselves into the game by making a call about whether someone stepped out of bounds. That's all well and good. But you aren't playing in the game.)

In politics, baby steps are often necessary. No prominent Republican politician running for president or any other high-profile office is going to come out in favor of some sort of comprehensive immigration reform plan at this point. But there are a few things that could happen that might well help Republicans take the first steps of a reconciliation/courtship with the Hispanic community. Here are two that could happen between now and November.

## 1. TURN DOWN THE RHETORIC

There's lots and lots of heat, rhetorically speaking, around the issue of immigration—legal and illegal—within the GOP. And there's a simple reason for it: it works. Arizona governor Jan Brewer is a perfect example. Prior to her decision to sign the nation's most restrictive immigration law in the country in 2010, Brewer was in deep trouble in both a primary and a general election. In the aftermath of the bill being signed, she became a national conservative hero, and her primary opponents dropped out in a nod to the political reality that she was unbeatable. Ditto the general election, where she cruised to victory despite a formidable Democratic nominee. The presidential nominee needs to send a signal that the party is done with throwing around inflammatory rhetoric as a cheap ploy to win votes from the base. That's not to say that the nominee has to disavow the need for the border to be secure and other tenets of the conservative position on immigration. Instead, the nominee has to make clear that the party needs to find a new and better way to talk about it.

This sort of rhetorical shift isn't entirely unprecedented when it comes to presidential politics. Remember that Bill Clinton repositioned the Democratic Party in the 1990s on the issue of abortion, which he recognized was a political loser for his side, by emphasizing the fact that he, like most Americans, believed it should be "safe, legal, and rare." That construction didn't change the basic pro-choice position of the Democratic Party but it did reframe the issue in a way that made it more acceptable to independents and even some moderate Republicans to vote for Clinton. It was a position that reflected where the public was on the issue: no one liked abortions but most people didn't want to see them outlawed either.

That's the very same trick that Republicans need to pull on immigration. They need to acknowledge that no one likes the fact that so many people are in the country illegally and that the border needs to be secured, while de-emphasizing their belief that the eleven million people who are here illegally need to be sent home. Politics is about finding ways to mold your core beliefs to those of the constituencies you are trying to woo. Republicans desperately need to do that when it comes to immigration.

## 2. PICK A HISPANIC VICE PRESIDENT

No, putting a Hispanic on the national ticket doesn't solve Republicans' problems with Latinos any more than having a black roommate means that you aren't a racist. But it's a start. It's a foothold. And Republicans desperately need both in the Hispanic community.

Putting a Hispanic in a position of such prominence wouldn't change where the Republican Party stands—and has stood—on the issue of immigration. But it would almost certainly earn the party a second look from many (though not all) within the Hispanic community. Hearing one of their own articulate why he or she decided to be a Republican is far more likely to be persuasive to Hispanics than hearing an old white guy make the case for the Grand Old—emphasis on old—Party.

It would also be a historic pick, which allows the party to counter the historic nature of President Obama. And a look back at recent vice presidential picks suggests that a sense of history is perhaps the most powerful driving force behind how the choice gets made. In 2008,

John McCain and his senior political team badly wanted to dilute the historic vote edge that Obama had as the first African American to win a major party's presidential nomination. Picking Sarah Palin made sense within that context, matching history with history. (Obviously, the practical reality of putting Palin on the ticket worked out considerably less well for McCain.) And, in 2000, Al Gore's decision to make Connecticut senator Joe Lieberman the first Jewish person on a national ticket drew him scads of positive publicity nationwide and almost certainly helped Gore in Florida—though not enough.

It's difficult to overestimate the pride of a community when one of their own breaks a long-held glass ceiling in American public life. (Need evidence? Look at the massive turnout and consolidation of the black vote behind Barack Obama in both the primary and general election in 2008.)

The good thing for the Republican Party is it has a number of Hispanics now in prominent statewide positions from which to pick. While there are 1,380 Hispanic Democrats in elected office nationwide and just 158 Hispanic Republicans, the GOP has gained twenty-nine seats since the 2006 election while Democrats have lost twenty-five over that same time period.

The conversation about a Hispanic vice presidential pick starts (and maybe ends) with Marco Rubio, the Senate sensation from Florida. That Rubio is Hispanic—Cuban, actually—is obviously a major helper for his chances. But he also brings two other major attributes that put him at the top of any Republican's vice presidential list.

First, he comes from Florida, a state that has been at the center of the fight for the presidency for the last decade. While putting Rubio on the ticket wouldn't ensure a Florida win for Republicans, he is a popular figure in the state and would undoubtedly narrow—if not entirely erase—the Democrats' edge among Hispanic voters in the Sunshine State. In his 2010 Senate race, Rubio won 45 percent of the Hispanic vote and 48 percent of the white vote in a three-way general election contest. (Representative Kendrick Meek was the Democratic nominee, and then governor Charlie Crist ran as an independent.)

Second, and of equal importance, is the fact that Rubio is an absolute darling of the Tea Party movement. His rapid rise against popular (and moderate) Crist in the 2010 Senate primary was the first tangible evidence that the Tea Party had real political power. Since his victory, Rubio has been touted as a leader of the movement by the national media and feted at conservative confabs like CPAC. (Al Cardenas, a former chairman of the Florida Republican Party, introduced Rubio at CPAC 2012, noting that he is "someone I know I'm going to say hello to at 1600 Pennsylvania Avenue someday.")

Combine those three factors—Hispanic, Florida, and Tea Party—and it's clear why Rubio is the heavy front-runner to be the vice presidential pick. But if for whatever reason he winds up not being the choice—stranger things have happened—Republicans have several other credible Hispanic alternatives.

One is Susana Martinez, who was elected governor of New Mexico—swing state alert!—in 2010. Martinez beat the sitting Democratic lieutenant governor by nearly eight points to become the first Hispanic woman elected governor—by either party—in the country. Her tough-on-crime credentials—she served as the district attorney in Dona Ana County prior to winning the governorship—coupled with the fact that she hails from a swing southwestern state makes her a potentially appealing choice for a Republican Party looking to reach out to Hispanics.

Another name that will likely be mentioned in the veepstakes is Nevada governor Brian Sandoval, who swept to his current office in 2010 by winning 33 percent of Hispanic voters and a remarkable 62 percent of whites. (It didn't hurt Sandoval's appeal to white voters that Rory Reid, the son of the unpopular Senate majority leader, was the Democratic nominee.) Sandoval's résumé is mighty impressive. He was elected attorney general in Nevada in 2002, and President

George W. Bush appointed him three years later as a United States district judge. He left that lifetime appointment behind to run for governor of Nevada. And, like Florida and New Mexico, Nevada is a major swing state in 2012, making Sandoval an even more attractive pick.

# THE 2016 POLITICAL ALL-STAR GAME STARTERS

Over the years in covering campaign politics, I developed a foolproof test for separating the truest of political junkies from the merely politically "interested." The test is simple: in the midst of a hotly contested presidential campaign—like this one—I mention what the next presidential race in four years' time might look like. Political passersby say something to the effect of "Can't we finish this race first?" True political junkies immediately get a sort of faraway look in their eyes and an excitement in their voice as they contemplate all of the possibilities that the race beyond the current one holds. Those are my people. And this one is for you.

There are any number of ways to tackle who the true rising stars in each party are and will be, the people who will populate *The Gospel*

*According to The Fix* 2016 edition. But I always tend to return to the world of sports for my inspiration, since sports is all about the unending search for new talent, finding the next big thing before he or she becomes the next big thing. Given that, I thought about doing the political equivalent of an NBA Draft—going through the top twenty (or so) picks in each party that someone looking to build a political dynasty would select. But then my editor said a draft didn't work. (Damn editors!) And right around that time, I read an extended riff by Bill Simmons about the NBA All-Star game—who should start, who shouldn't, and why. Lightbulb! So below are my starting lineups for the 2016 political all-star game. I would actually love to see these ten people on a court together playing a game of pickup hoops. But, I digress . . .

There are caveats everywhere when you try to see four years into the future. The most obvious is that, well, shit happens in politics. Mark Sanford, the disgraced former governor of South Carolina, might have made this list in 2008. Former New York governor Eliot Spitzer (D-escorts) would definitely have been on it. So, things change. Another caveat: the 2012 Republican vice presidential sweepstakes, which is only in its infancy as I write these words, will surely have something to say about the starting five for the Republican side. If someone not on our list below happens to be the vice presidential pick—always a possibility—he or she would, obviously, have a spot on the 2016 starting five, unless the GOP ticket imploded between now and November. Caveats dispatched.

*Ladies and gentlemen, your 2016 political all-star game starters! Representing the Republican Party . . .*

## . . . A FRESHMAN SENATOR FROM FLORIDA, MARCO RUBIOOOOOOO

If we did do a political draft—in your face, editor!—Rubio would be the consensus number one pick. He's got all the tangibles (Hispanic, swing state, Tea Party darling) and lots of the intangibles too (a gifted speaker, charismatic, seemingly regular guy appeal). Rubio is the LeBron James of this all-star game; he has all the tools to be one of the greats. But, like LeBron, Rubio has coasted through his political life a little bit too easily and has some holes in his game that he still needs to address. The biggest is his tendency to play slightly fast and loose with his personal biography. The *Washington Post* dinged him in 2011 by noting that his oft-recounted story that his parents had fled the rule of Fidel Castro was in fact not true; his parents left Cuba more than two years before Castro came to power in 1959. Rubio acknowledged the discrepancy but downplayed it, insisting that it was the result of being told incorrect information in the "oral history" of his family. Rubio also had some trouble during his 2010 Senate race regarding questionable charges on a state party credit card, including six plane tickets for his wife. ("My wife was the first lady of the Florida House of Representatives, and it is absolutely appropriate for her to accompany me to official events and party functions," Rubio said at the time, explaining the charges. Florida's statehouse has a first lady? Who knew!) Still, in spite of those slight weaknesses, Rubio is still the most complete player on the floor in 2016.

## THE GOVERNOR OF LOUISIANA, BOBBY JINDAL

If the timing had worked out slightly better for Jindal in 2012, we could well be talking about him as the presidential nominee this time around. (Jindal was up for reelection to a second term in November 2011, making it logistically impossible for him to also run for president.) But Jindal, an Indian American who spent six years in the House before being elected as governor of the Bayou State in 2007, has all the tools to make a serious run at the top job in 2016. He's a popular figure in Louisiana and has built a governing record centered on reform—from ethics to education. If he can put together a second term as well regarded as his first, Jindal could challenge Rubio for top dog honors on the 2016 court. Jindal detractors will, rightly, note that in his debut on the national stage—the 2009 Republican response to President Obama's address to a joint session of Congress—he bombed. Speaking from the foyer of the Louisiana governor's mansion, Jindal looked hokey as hell. His singsongy voice, which drew unfavorable comparisons to Kenneth the Page from NBC's *30 Rock*, didn't help matters. The question for Jindal is whether that was a blip on the radar or a sign of bigger problems scaling up to the national stage. (Is he J. J. Redick, a dominant college force but a role player in the NBA?) Writing off Jindal—or even de-valuing his upside—based on a single performance is a major mistake. This guy has the goods—in a major way.

## THE GOVERNOR OF SOUTH CAROLINA, NIKKI HALEY

Haley became a national figure for all the wrong reasons in 2010. Just as she appeared to be surging in the South Carolina gubernatorial primary, a prominent Republican blogger in the state went public with an allegation that he had engaged in an extramarital affair with her. It became national news immediately, and conservatives—including the one and only Sarah Palin—rushed to her defense, casting her as the victim of a smear campaign. Haley vehemently denied the charges and went on TV with an ad featuring her husband and two children that urged South Carolinians to move past the state's history of viciously brutal campaigns. She became a sympathetic figure and cruised to a victory in both the primary and general election, making her the first Indian American woman to be elected governor in the country. Haley, who built a reputation as a reformer during her time in the state senate and was a onetime political protégée of Mark Sanford (oops!), has struggled somewhat in her first two years in office to push her agenda through the

Republican-controlled state legislature. She also chose the wrong horse—Mitt Romney—to back in the state's first-in-the-South presidential primary. But Haley is charismatic, conservative, and from a critical state in the nominating process.

## THE GOVERNOR OF NEW JERSEY, CHRIS CHRISTIE

When Christie won the governorship of the Garden State in 2009—the first Republican to do so since Christine Todd Whitman in 1997—few national political observers had high hopes for him. After all, he had never before served in elected office and had been heavily advantaged in the race by the incredible high negatives of the incumbent—New Jersey governor Jon Corzine (D). And then there was the unspoken doubt about Christie: could a man who was, by his own admission, obese ever become a major national figure in the world of cable television? Christie's answer to all those doubters? Go fuck yourself. Well, not literally. But damn close. Christie's no-nonsense approach to politics and the political media—his confrontation with a Newark *Star-Ledger* columnist early in his term became the stuff of conservative legend and has been viewed by tens of thousands on YouTube—made him a breakout star nationally. Christie was the toast of the conservative community and repeatedly had to beat back rumors that he was thinking of running for president in 2012. His endorsement of Mitt Romney was one of the few endorsements that might have mattered in the Republican race. All of that ensures Christie a starting spot on our 2016 all-star team. While Christie's natural political talent is immense, there are some lingering issues for him that came up during the 2009 race—most notably a $46,000 loan he gave to a female underling during his tenure as the U.S. attorney in New Jersey. Christie's decision as governor to take a state-sponsored helicopter ride to his son's baseball game also suggests that he might have grown a little too impressed with his positive press and convinced himself that he could do no wrong politically. (After initially refusing to reimburse the state for the use of the helicopter, Christie caved and decided to pay it back.) None of those problems keep Christie off the court in our 2016 game though. Yes, he has weaknesses. But his natural strengths more than make up for them. The question for Christie is whether he is Dwight Howard (massive physical gifts and an amazing player) or Kwame Brown (massive physical gifts and not an amazing player).

## THE GOVERNOR OF VIRGINIA, BOB McDONNELL

McDonnell's election in the swing state of Virginia in 2009 was touted by national Republicans as the first major sign that the Obama wave that had swept the country—and the Commonwealth of Virginia—in 2008 had finally begun to recede. McDonnell, who had spent four years as the state's attorney general before running for governor, put together a very disciplined campaign that focused almost exclusively on his plan to create jobs for Virginians. (Yard signs touting BOB'S FOR JOBS were everywhere, even in the more liberal northern Virginia suburbs in the days and weeks leading up to the 2009 vote.) His closing of a more than $4 billion state budget shortfall and an unemployment rate well below the national average have highlighted McDonnell's first several years in office. He's been rewarded by voters with more than six in ten approving of the job he is doing, unheard-of numbers at a time when politicians are incredibly unpopular as a general rule. Another helper for McDonnell: Virginia is regarded by strategists of both parties as the swingiest of the swing states, and putting a popular governor on the national ticket could be enough to sway a very close contest. McDonnell's closest analog in the world of professional basketball? Probably Russell Westbrook of the Oklahoma City Thunder. Both have lots of natural gifts and both, occasionally, don't use them as they should. Westbrook shoots too much. McDonnell follows his social conservative roots—he got in the middle of a fight over transvaginal ultrasounds in the spring—a bit too often.

## THE FORMER GOVERNOR OF FLORIDA, JEB BUSH

At the start of the 2012 election, most analysts thought that the country simply wasn't ready for another Bush in the White House. After all, George W. Bush had left office with dismal approval ratings, and the Bush name—once so golden in American politics—was decidedly tarnished. But as the race played itself out, it became clear that any lingering concerns about the former Florida governor's last name were more than made up for by his status as a big thinker in a field filled with small ones. That's why Bush is on the court in 2016 if he wants to be. He is a major figure of substance on everything from immigration to education in a party that may well be desperate for that sort of profile. He is also someone who ended his eight years in office as one of the most popular elected officials in the swing state of Florida and someone whose last name means he would never want for campaign cash or organization. The question always with Jeb is: What does he want? He plays his political cards very close to the vest and has seemed largely uninterested in wading into the nitty-gritty of politics since leaving office in 2006. Bush, almost certainly, would like to get the nomination by acclamation in 2016, but that's just not going to happen. There are too many other ambitious people who simply won't step aside for him. Bush is like Michael Jordan during his baseball sabbatical. When he came back to playing hoops, everyone tested Jordan—trying to figure out whether he was really the old MJ or not. That's exactly what would happen if Bush decided to run in 2016 or 2020. Is Bush willing to prove himself all over again? Or would he rather retire to a skybox and watch the proceedings unfold from afar?

## SIXTH MAN, JOHN THUNE

Out of our Republican team, Thune is the best basketball player of the bunch. (He played college basketball at the Biblical Institute of Los Angeles.) And, on paper, he's a great prospect: he took out then Senate majority leader Tom Daschle in 2004, he is very well liked by social conservatives, and his home state shares a border with Iowa (and its first-in-the-nation caucuses). Thune is also personable, charismatic, and handsome; he looks like what you might find if you typed "presidential candidate" into an online dictionary. Thune's problem is that campaigns aren't run on paper, and there are lingering questions about how much heart he has for a bruising race where the outcome is far from guaranteed. Thune backed away from the 2012 contest with a whimper, despite the fact that there was a relatively clear path for him into the top tier of the field. He is clearly a candidate with significant gifts. But he is also someone who has proven reluctant to gamble with those gifts. Thune is now a member of the Senate Republican leadership team and may well decide he'd rather climb the ladder toward minority/majority leader than risk it all on a presidential bid. Thune has been great out of the limelight. He's got all the tools—à la Carmelo Anthony—but 'Melo seems to have shrunk a bit since moving from the Denver Nuggets to the New York Knicks. Can Thune perform when the national spotlight is shining on him? It's an open question. But he still gets a spot on our team—based on his potential alone.

*And now for your Democratic starters . . .*

## . . . THE GOVERNOR OF NEW YORK, ANDREW CUOMO

Cuomo's last name alone—he is the son of former Empire State governor Mario Cuomo, the unrequited love of many Democratic presidential observers—puts him on the floor for 2016. His résumé is what makes him the unquestioned floor leader. Cuomo spent most of the 1990s working in the Clinton administration, first as the assistant secretary of housing and urban development and then—in Clinton's second term—as the housing and urban development secretary. His political rise hit a bit of a bump in 2002 when he entered the Democratic primary for governor leading in the polls but wound up dropping out of the race just before the September primary when it became clear he had no chance of winning. Cuomo regrouped, however, and ran successfully for state attorney general in 2006 and then cruised to the state's top job in 2010. Cuomo drew credit from both parties for pushing through a 2011 budget that didn't raise taxes. He burst into the national spotlight when he helped shepherd the state's same-sex-marriage law to passage, a major boost for his liberal bona fides (and bank account) if and when he decides to pull the trigger on a presidential bid. David B. Mixner, a longtime gay rights advocate and major player in Democratic politics, told the *New York Times* that Cuomo "made himself a national player, almost with one piece of legislation, and that's not going to change." The question for Cuomo is whether he's learned the lessons of his failed 2002 bid, when he came off as an entitled know-it-all; his victories since that race suggest he has, and if that's true, Cuomo's the odds-on favorite to be the party's presidential nominee in 2016. Cuomo's obvious basketball comparison is Kobe Bryant. Both men had dads who played the game. Both have experienced failure and worked to make sure it never happens again. And both are among the most Machiavellian characters in their respective worlds.

## THE GOVERNOR OF MARYLAND, MARTIN O'MALLEY

Familiarity can breed contempt or, at least, disinterest. And that's definitely the case for the national media when it comes to O'Malley, whose proximity to the nation's capital—and the thousands of political reporters who call it home—means he is probably undercovered as a potential national candidate. O'Malley has a terrific story to tell as the mayor of a major American city and a two-term governor in a strongly Democratic state. (During his time as mayor of Baltimore, he was named by *Time* magazine as one of the five best big-city mayors in the country.) He also has some intangibles—he sings and plays guitar in an Irish band, he's good-looking—that will help at the margins as voters look for the next big thing in Democratic politics. O'Malley is also part politician, part political operative; he started in politics as an advance guy for Colorado senator Gary Hart's presidential bid and now runs the Democratic Governors Association, an organization solely tasked with adding to the number of Democrats in statewide office around the country. O'Malley is sort of like a Chris Bosh–type player in the race; he's overshadowed by the Cuomos and, yes, Clintons but is a proven commodity who can even surprise you if you don't keep close track of him. He's sneaky good.

## THE SENATOR FROM VIRGINIA, MARK WARNER

If Bob McDonnell isn't the most popular politician in the Commonwealth of Virginia, it's only because of Warner. Warner is a self-made millionaire (and more), thanks to being an early adopter and investor in a little thing called cellular telephones. (Warner was involved back when cell phones looked like that massive thing Gordon Gekko toted around in *Wall Street*.) After running unsuccessfully for Senate in 1996—a race no one thought he had a chance in and where he did surprisingly well—Warner bided his time and then ran for governor in 2001. His victory was the first by a Democrat since Doug Wilder won the office in 1989 and featured not only a brand-new coalition for the party that was based in the vote-rich northern Virginia suburbs but also included traditionally conservative areas in the southwestern part of the state that were drawn to Warner's jobs and technology messaging. In office, Warner pulled off the impossible—forging agreement with a Republican legislature on a $1.3 billion tax increase plan in order to balance the commonwealth's budget. Warner's popularity only grew after he was term limited out of office in 2005. He was widely expected to run for president in 2008 but unexpectedly bowed out of the race in late 2006 for—still—unexplained reasons. Instead of running for president, Warner sought the state's open U.S. Senate seat in 2008 and won with 65 percent—a remarkable showing in a state so closely divided along partisan lines. Warner's considerable personal wealth and electoral success in a swing state recommend him as a candidate. His centrist politics, however, could complicate his future on the national stage, since voters who are to Warner's ideological left will almost certainly control the nomination fight. Warner has a bit of an odd political game; he's sort of like Shawn Marion of the Dallas Mavericks. His style isn't polished to a gleam and his politics are well short of what liberals want. And yet he just keeps finding ways to win—overwhelmingly—in a swing state.

## ELIZABETH WARREN

Yes, we realize the (somewhat) ridiculous notion of putting someone on our 2016 all-star starting five who hasn't even been elected—and may not be elected—yet. But Warren is an exception worth making. The former Harvard Law professor came to national prominence as a co-chair of the congressional committee overseeing the disbursement of money from the Troubled Asset Relief Program (TARP). She was also instrumental in the creation of the Consumer Financial Protection Bureau—although her liberal views made her impossible to be confirmed (and President Obama didn't even try) as the head of the newly formed agency. Over that time, Warren became a cult hero among the liberal left, a status only bolstered by her decision to challenge Senator Scott Brown (R) in November for the seat once held by the late Ted Kennedy. Warren's fund-raising prowess in the race is eye-popping—she collected more than $9 million in her first four months as a candidate in 2011—and if she can beat Brown she will immediately become a national star on the Democratic side. To those who say she is too inexperienced to possibly be considered for a presidential bid, we have two words for you: *Barack Obama*. When 2016 rolls around, Warren, if elected, will have spent three years in the Senate—exactly the amount of time Obama was in the world's greatest deliberative body before pursuing the presidency. It could well be déjà vu all over again. Warren's closest comparison in basketball is Anthony Davis, the eighteen-year-old wunderkind who led Kentucky to an NCAA Championship in 2012. Everyone expects him to be a terrific pro, but he's not in the league just yet. When he gets there, he'll start to dominate.

## THE MAYOR OF CHICAGO, RAHM EMANUEL

Every team needs an enforcer—someone who not only relishes the back and forth of the game but also excels at it. That's Emanuel. After spending years in the political arm of the Clinton White House, Emanuel sought elected office on his own in 2002, running for and winning the open Fifth District seat of Illinois. (The seat was vacated by then representative Rod Blagojevich, who went on to become governor of the state and then a convicted felon. But that's another book.) Six years later, after overseeing the Democratic takeover of the House in 2006, Emanuel was plucked from office by an offer to become President Obama's first White House chief of staff. He left that post in 2010 to pursue his self-described dream job of mayor of Chicago. Emanuel's opponents insisted he wasn't eligible to run because he hadn't lived in the state for the past two years. Emanuel rode over them—and their objections—to win the mayor's office easily. While he dismisses talk of a Senate or gubernatorial bid in the future, people as ambitious as Emanuel don't just turn off the switch. They can't. And so Rahm will almost certainly continue to make moves—both in Illinois and, eventually, on a national stage. Might he be our first Jewish president? Emanuel reminds me most of John Stockton, the Hall of Fame point guard for the Utah Jazz. Stockton was a great player and facilitator—he always got his teammates involved—but also had a reputation for walking right up to the line of being a dirty player.

## AND THE SIXTH (WO)MAN, SECRETARY OF STATE HILLARY CLINTON

I believe Clinton when she says that when she leaves the secretary of state's office at the end of this year that she will be totally and completely done with politics. After all, she's spent more than three decades in the public eye and has withstood more scrutiny and criticism than anyone else we can think of. Clinton is well within her rights to declare that she is simply done with the world of politics. And yet . . . she will be only sixty-eight years old (Ronald Reagan was sixty-nine when he was first elected) in November 2016 and, by all accounts, has plenty of vim and vigor left in her. What remains unknown is how hindsight has affected Clinton's thinking about her 2008 bid. Does she view it as her one shot to run for president that, for a variety of reasons, failed? Or does she view it as a job left undone? If it's the latter then she could well have one more run in her. Obviously if Clinton did get into the 2016 race, she would effectively function as the prime mover—the person around which all of the other candidates would rotate. Again, this is *not* the most likely—or even close to a likely—scenario. But it's also impossible to know whether Hillary Clinton is truly done with politics just yet. If she feels like 2008 left her with some unfinished business, 2016 might be her chance to write the final chapter of her political life—with a happier ending. Who is Clinton in our political hoops game? Magic Johnson? Larry Bird? One of the two. She's part of political royalty. She's the sort of politician all other politicians defer to when they are in a group. She's got "it"—whatever "it" is.

# CAMPAIGN FINANCE REFORM— IN ONE SIMPLE STEP

CUE MATTHEW LESKO (THE GUY WITH THE QUES-
TION MARK SUIT COAT): Hey everybody! Don't we all agree
that there is TOO much money in politics!

CROWD: YEAH!

LESKO: Of course we do. We all know that politicians are bought
and paid for by the people giving them money. And what about us
poor saps who don't have the money to give? We're left out in the
cold!

CROWD: Booooooo!

LESKO: So, how do we get all the money out of politics? We don't!
You've got to live in the real world, people! Money will always find

its way into politics. Wealthy people want to use their dollars to gain access and influence over the men and women in positions of political power. It's always been that way. It's always going to be that way.

WOMAN IN CROWD: So, what the heck can we do about it?

LESKO: Funny you should ask. Because I've got a solution. Let's start with the idea that political money is like energy—it's never created nor destroyed just transferred. Don't believe me? Two years after McCain-Feingold—the law that was going to finally take money out of politics—a relatively small group of Democratic strategists and donors formed a three-headed shadow Democratic Party that raised and spent $160 million in an all-out effort to defeat President Bush. NEWSFLASH: It failed. Then came super PACs—love that name, folks!—that cropped up after the Supreme Court made its *Citizens United* ruling . . .

*[Crowd members begin to whisper among themselves, clearly losing interest]*

LESKO: OK, OK. So you don't want to know about court cases. Fine! Here's the point. People can give to super PACs—as much as they want for as long as they want. Super PACs can spend that money telling you and your friends to vote for or against a candidate. The people with the deep pockets have the loudest voices. But THERE IS ANOTHER WAY . . .

*[Crowd leans in, anticipating the big idea]*

LESKO: . . . and it's so simple. Ready? You can give as much as you want to any candidate. But if you give $10,000, you have to put your name and your employer online within twenty-four hours of the donation. HOW ABOUT THAT, FOLKS! IS THAT A GAME-CHANGER OR WHAT?

CROWD: [Polite applause]

OK. So campaign finance reform is not the sort of sexy topic that a man of Lesko's massive infomercial gifts should be wasted on. But the idea presented above is simple enough that it just might work. Here's why.

The technology already exists. Campaigns already have to electronically file donations received in the final week before a primary within forty-eight hours. Outside groups have to file any money they are spending on campaigns within twenty-four hours of doing it. All of this electronic disclosure goes through the Federal Election Commission. The FEC already has a system in place to handle just this sort of rapid disclosure. And because the bar for immediate disclosure would be $10,000, the FEC wouldn't be overwhelmed with the logistical nightmare of trying to rapidly post thousands of $50 contributions.

What would immediate disclosure accomplish? It would allow a light to shine—brightly and quickly—on who was funding the various groups trying to influence the political process. More specifically, it would allow reporters—like me—to dig into the funders and write stories about who they are, what their ties are to the candidate, and even why they might be giving. Immediate disclosure would force donors to think twice about whether they wanted their name in lights—or at least in media reports—as soon as they cut a check. (At the moment, a donor can write a check in the beginning of the year and, depending on the reporting requirements, not have that donation publicly available for six months or longer.) That could well cut down on the amount of money moving through the political system, as there will be some donors who, for a variety of reasons, would prefer not to draw that kind of attention to themselves.

The more light shone on the activities of these outside groups, the more likely it is that the American public—or at least those who read blogs and newspapers or watch cable news—will be better informed about the various groups trying to persuade them for or against a candidate and, theoretically, better able to make a good decision about the information they are being fed through television and radio ads.

Not only would immediate disclosure satisfy the campaign finance reform types who are forever pushing for more transparency in the process, but it would also be a hard thing for those opposed to reforming the political fund-raising system to block. The main push back against any sort of campaign finance reform is that it amounts to a restriction on free speech. Well, this proposal would allow anyone to give as much money as he/she liked. The only reason to not support it would be because of the immediate disclosure requirements, which, of course, have nothing to do with free speech.

One other potential benefit from putting an immediate disclosure provision into law? It could well lessen the influence of so-called non-profit groups—known as 501c3s and 501c4s—which have burgeoned over the past decade in the political process. These groups do not have any—I repeat, any—disclosure requirements, meaning that they can raise and spend millions of dollars without ever making public who's giving to them or how much they are giving. The downside of these groups is that they can't directly advocate for or against a candidate and instead have to run issue-based campaigns. Wouldn't some donors, who don't mind being a bit more public with their giving, jump at the chance to see their money used to directly influence elections?

We could start slowly. Maybe test the $10,000 immediate disclosure requirement for the 2016 presidential primary season. (Sort of like how the Big East tried out the idea of a six-fouls limit back in the mid 2000s.) If it works and accomplishes its goal of heightened transparency, it could be expanded to the presidential general election in 2016 and then to all federal races in 2018.

Maybe immediate disclosure isn't the final—or only, or best—answer when it comes to reforming the way in which campaigns are funded. But unlike many of the reforms being pushed nowadays, it would deal with the way politics is, not the way some people would like it to be. Money and politics will forever be linked. The key is to expose to the public those ties that bind and let them make the decision about whether it's a good thing or a bad thing. That is, after all, how democracy is supposed to work, right?

# THE
# SUPER PAC
# WHISPERER

You've probably never heard of Carl Forti. He's rarely been on television and he's rarely quoted in the newspaper. But Forti knows the world of super PACs better than anyone in the Republican Party—and that knowledge makes him one of most important strategists in the country heading into the fall election.

Before you get to know Forti, you need to get to know super PACs. Outside money has been spent on campaigns for as long as there have been campaigns. Wealthy individuals interested in politics have long sought ways around the relatively stringent federal campaign finance regulations—you can only donate $2,500 or so to a candidate—in hopes of exerting more influence on the electoral process.

In the early part of the 2000s, the spending vehicle of choice was known as a 527, which referred to the section of the tax code that governed its operations. The 527s could raise unlimited amounts of money from individuals, but the groups had to disclose the names and donation amounts of everyone who gave to them. The 527s also couldn't directly advocate for the election or defeat of a candidate. What does that mean in real life? A 527 could run an ad highlighting

John Kerry's flip-flops on the war in Iraq. It couldn't explicitly say that those flip-flops were a reason not to vote for him. It's a subtle difference but an important one.

All of that changed in 2010 with the much ballyhooed *Citizens United* ruling by the Supreme Court. *Citizens United* did lots of things to change campaign finance law in the country, but the most significant one was that it got rid of the ban on outside groups expressly advocating for the election or defeat of a candidate. From that ruling super PACs were born, political committees free to accept unlimited donations and directly advocate for or against a candidate. (Super PACs, like 527s, do have to disclose their donors and the amount of each contribution.) If *Citizens United* was the parent, the super PAC was the golden child. And Forti was the one who first recognized that the child was a political prodigy.

When I met Forti more than a decade ago, I would not have bet that he would become the man who would rock the political world. He was a big guy—a prototypical power forward in pickup hoops—who, in meetings, would almost always be sitting quietly in the corner with a bemused smirk on his face. (If you looked up *palooka* in the dictionary, you got Forti.) In those days—circa 2000—Forti was working as the communications director at the National Republican Congressional Committee, a job of considerable import within Washington—the NRCC is responsible for electing Republican candidates to the U.S. House—but with virtually no profile outside of Washington. (Little did I know what a talent incubator the NRCC was in those days; the political director, Terry Nelson, went on to manage Senator John McCain's 2008 presidential campaign for a time.)

Forti stayed with the NRCC for a total of four elections. By the 2006 elections he was not just managing the communications operation but he was also running a vast independent expenditure program—under another quirk of campaign finance law, the party committees could run television ads in hopes of influencing the outcomes—that eventually spent more than $80 million. (All of that spending did Forti—and the GOP—little good in the 2006 election; Democrats won back the House after twelve years in the wilderness of the minority.) Forti left that gig to move to Boston and serve as the political director of Mitt Romney's 2008 presidential campaign. "Why would you want to talk to me?" Forti remembers asking the Romney team, noting that all of his experience was on the communications side, not the political side. The response? "You get shit done."

When Romney went kaput in the presidential race, Forti moved back to Virginia and started his own consulting business known as the Black Rock Group. (The firm was named after Black Rock, New York—a neighbor to Forti's native Buffalo.) And that's when things started happening for Forti in the world of super PACs.

It all began with American Crossroads, a super PAC organized around the 2010 election and designed to help Republicans win House and Senate seats. Bush administration political svengali Karl Rove and longtime Republican operative Steven Law were the other two foundational pillars of Crossroads. (They raised the money, he spent it, Forti explained.) American Crossroads grew into a fund-raising behemoth and a Democratic nightmare.

For the 2010 election, Crossroads raised and spent $71 million on House and Senate races, a massive sum that helped tip control of the lower chamber to Republicans and aided the party's six-seat pickup in the Senate. And Crossroads didn't let up, raising a massive $51 million in 2011 and doubling—yes, doubling—its initial $100 million fund-raising goal for 2012 to $200 million.

Even as Crossroads was taking off, Forti as well as a few other Romney loyalists formed a super PAC known as Restore Our Future designed to help the former Massachusetts governor win the Republican presidential nomination in 2012. And help him they did. Restore Our Future collected $30 million in 2011 alone and used those millions on an all-out assault on Newt Gingrich that blunted the momentum the former House Speaker was building in late 2011 and early 2012 and allowed Romney to secure much-needed victories in New Hampshire, Florida, and Nevada.

As of early March 2012, 371 super PACs had raised more than $130 million (!) in the 2012 election. The mightiest were those affiliated with Republican presidential candidates. Restore Our Future led the way, with $34 million collected, followed by Winning Our Future, a super PAC aligned with former House Speaker Newt Gingrich that had raised $16 million—almost all of which came from the personal checkbook of casino magnate Sheldon Adelson.

Adelson's largesse directed to Gingrich is evidence of just how much super PACs have changed the political calculus in the less than two years they have been in existence. During the 2008 election, a candidate like Gingrich, who experienced very little success raising money for his official campaign account, would have been forced out of the presidential race months before he ultimately quit in early May—unable to pay his staff, travel the country, or run television ads.

But in the new super PAC world, Gingrich needed to convince only one very rich person—Adelson—of his continued viability in the race. Beginning in January, Adelson has cut a series of multimillion-dollar checks to Winning Our Future, which was run by—surprise, surprise—a longtime Gingrich staffer named Rick Tyler. Those donations paid for thousands of television ads in South Carolina, which Gingrich won in late January, and helped him secure a victory in his home state of Georgia on March 6.

Without Sheldon Adelson, Gingrich is an afterthought in the 2012 presidential race. With him, Gingrich remained a viable candidate all the way through the middle of March. That's how drastically super PACs have changed the landscape on which the presidential race is being fought.

The White House was paying close attention to the tens of millions of dollars pouring into Republican super PACs in the first few months of 2012. And they were getting worried. So in February the White House publicly reversed its stated opposition to such groups. In an e-mail sent to supporters, Obama campaign manager Jim Messina argued that the move was born of necessity: "We decided to do this because we can't afford for the work you're doing in your communities, and the grassroots donations you give to support it, to be destroyed by hundreds of millions of dollars in negative ads," he wrote.

What secret has Forti figured out that inspired such fear in the White House? He insists there is no secret, and if he knows one, he certainly isn't telling. He attributes his success to "keeping my head down and doing my job," adding: "I'm not a self-promoter. I'm not on TV all the time." (What's wrong with being on TV all the time? But I digress . . .)

Forti's preference to be behind the scenes rather than in front of the camera may hold the key to understanding why he has been affiliated with the two most successful super PACs on record. These organizations function on privacy; donors are the most skittish of political animals and need to know that the people whom they are dealing with can keep a secret. (Donors also want to know their money is being well

The Obama political team made a very simple political calculation. They could reverse course, take the near-term hit from campaign finance reform advocates and reap the long-term financial benefits, or stay the course and run the risk of being outspent in 2012. Viewed that way, the decision was a no-brainer and had echoes of Obama's decision in 2008 to go back on his promise to abide by public financing once it became clear that he could dramatically outraise Senator John McCain in the fall election. His Republican critics lambast Obama as an ideologue, but decisions like the one on super PACs make clear that he is, at heart, a political pragmatist. Which, of course, is why he's in the White House right now.

spent or they will stop giving, said Forti. "You can't convince these folks to give the type of money they are giving if they don't think they are having an impact," he added.) Forti's great gift then is his discretion. He is a vault and donors—and the staffers he works with—know it. That's why they tell him things and give him money. And that's why he's the super PAC whisperer.

# THE FIX POLITICAL HALL OF FAME

One of my favorite childhood memories growing up in Connecticut was taking the drive up I-91 north to Springfield, Massachusetts, to go to the Basketball Hall of Fame. They had Shaq's giant shoes, hoops that you could shoot on, and stats galore. Ditto Cooperstown, which I finally made it to when I was in college and my nerd status was in full bloom.

I always wondered why if basketball, baseball, and every other sport could have a shrine to the best that ever was, why couldn't politics have the same thing? After all, just like in sports, part of the appeal of politics is the ability to compare the successes (or failures) of people who were in office a hundred years ago with the men and women in elected office right now. If baseball could debate whether Ichiro Suzuki could hold a candle as a hitter to Joe DiMaggio (answer: no), then why couldn't politics have a place where junkies could argue about whether Bill Clinton could have beaten John Kennedy in a campaign?

Since no one was doing it, I made an executive decision to do it myself. Since I spend most of my existence (and do most of my writing) on the Internet—sort of like Max Headroom—I figured we should do a digital hall of fame rather than a brick and mortar one. (Also, there's no chance anyone would spend money—or at least give me money—for a national Political Hall of Fame. If we did have one, though, I think Massachusetts or Virginia would be good locations; both have produced lots and lots of presidential timber over the past few hundred years.)

Taking my cues from the Baseball Hall of Fame—still the best HOF there is—I decided to start the Political Hall of Fame with a five-member inaugural class. (The first five people into Cooperstown: Ty Cobb, Babe Ruth, Honus Wagner, Christy Mathewson, and Walter Johnson.)

The first five members of The Fix Political Hall of Fame are below. The Fix Political Hall of Fame Veterans Committee, which meets annually at Mount Rushmore, has already voted in Presidents Richard Nixon, Lyndon Johnson, Franklin Delano Roosevelt, and Abraham Lincoln—so they won't be mentioned here. Future editions of *The Gospel*—assuming, gulp, that they exist—will add more members.

## BILL CLINTON

When Bill Clinton was elected governor of Arkansas for the second time in 1982 (at age thirty-six), Michael Barone wrote the following passage about the boy governor in the *Almanac of American Politics:* "He presumably will avoid his earlier mistakes and not seek the national spotlight." Well, that didn't happen.

Clinton used the next decade to formulate his political philosophy, which would come to be encapsulated in the phrase "New Democrat," and hone his "aw shucks" charm and skills on the stump. Fast-forward to 1992. Clinton, still relatively unknown on the national stage, was given little chance of getting the party's presidential nomination in a field that included bigger names like former Massachusetts senator Paul Tsongas and former California governor Jerry Brown. Dogged by allegations of infidelity, Clinton somehow finished second in the New Hampshire primary, declared himself the "Comeback Kid," and ultimately took the nomination and—with an assist from independent candidate Ross Perot—the presidency.

Recounting the next eight years is worth a book—I'd recommend *The Survivor* by John F. Harris—but through all the ups and downs, Clinton always managed to persevere, the sign of a consummate politician.

During his wife's campaign for president in 2008, Clinton showed signs of wear and a lack of familiarity with how quickly an off-color comment could become national news in the Internet age. But in spite of those awkward growing pains, Clinton still showed flashes of brilliance. An example: days before the 2008 Iowa caucuses, Clinton arrived nearly an hour late to a speech in a high school gymnasium (The Fix was there). He took the stage and proceeded to speak for an hour without break to an enraptured audience, a remarkable performance that few politicians could ever hope to duplicate.

In the wake of that campaign, Clinton's approval ratings tanked—badly—as he lost the postpolitical shine that he had enjoyed since leaving the White House. But, true to form, Clinton quickly found a road back to popularity and now regularly enjoys approval ratings north of 60 percent.

The Clinton appeal as a politician is difficult to narrow down into a single trait, but if pressed I'd say it is centered on his fundamental humanness. Clinton is simultaneously the best that we all aspire to be (charismatic, brilliant, caring) and the worst (petty, prone to anger, philandering) parts that reside in each of us. He is us—with apologies to 2010 Delaware Senate candidate Christine O'Donnell—just more so, and played out on the grandest scale possible, the presidency of the United States. That Clinton prospered so much politically in spite of his considerable personal weaknesses is a testament to his natural gifts. And that's what makes him a member of our inaugural class.

# RONALD REAGAN

Reagan spent his early professional years as an actor—not exactly the most logical training for one of the best politicians in American history. (Or, in retrospect, maybe it was.) Elected head of the Screen Actors Guild in 1947 (he was nominated by Gene Kelly!), Reagan served in that role until 1951—a period dominated by the investigation of the House Un-American Activities Committee (HUAC) into alleged communism in Hollywood. Reagan became steadily more conservative during that time and increasingly interested in the political game. A decade later, he delivered an impassioned—and televised—speech in October 1964 on behalf of GOP presidential nominee Barry Goldwater that catapulted him into the national political spotlight. Two years after that, Reagan was elected governor of California, beating then governor Pat Brown.

By 1968, Reagan was a big enough player on the national stage to contemplate, but ultimately decide against, a run for the GOP presidential nomination. After winning a second term as governor in 1970, Reagan walked away from the chance to run for a third in 1974 and turned his attention to reshaping the Republican Party with a more conservative bent. He brought that new ideology to a surprisingly strong primary challenge to President Gerald Ford in 1976. Four years later, Reagan was the odds-on favorite for the nomination, and even though George H. W. Bush pushed him harder than expected in the primaries, Reagan won the nomination and then swamped President Jimmy Carter in November 1980 by winning 489 electoral votes. Reagan one-upped himself in his reelection bid, winning forty-nine states in a crushing defeat of Walter Mondale.

Reagan's second term was far less smooth than his first—due in large part to questions over his involvement in Iran-Contra—but he left office popular enough to see his vice president elected to the top job. Reagan departed from public life in 1994 following an announcement that he was suffering from Alzheimer's disease, but his legacy continues to exert considerable influence on the Republican Party.

Reagan's lasting influence in politics was his before-his-time understanding of the power of the bully pulpit and the way in which television could influence the national debate. Reagan understood in a sort of innate way that no matter what the newspapers wrote about him or the television anchors said about him, TV offered him a direct pipeline to the American people, which was the only constituency he—rightly—cared about. Reagan's ability to rise above—in the eyes of voters—the petty politics of Washington, from budget squabbles all the way to the Iran-Contra investigation, was the key to his success. Reagan used television—not to mention his carefully honed communication skills from his acting days and his years as the lead pitchman for General Electric—to speak directly to the American people in a way no one before him had done. And now, it's impossible to imagine a president *not* using television that way. Reagan changed the game. And for that he belongs in the Political Hall of Fame.

## TED KENNEDY

The youngest son of one of the most famous American families didn't really choose politics, he had politics thrust upon him. The baby of a family with nine children—love those Irish Catholics!—Kennedy watched as his older brothers Jack and Robert ascended to the heights of American politics.

Teddy was twenty-eight years old—and had already been kicked out of Harvard, served in the military, and returned to Cambridge to get his degree—when his brother Jack was elected president in 1960.

Two years later, Ted Kennedy was elected to the Massachusetts Senate seat from which he would carry on the liberal causes championed by his assassinated brothers and develop into one of the great legislators of his time—or any time.

To gloss over Kennedy's rough patches would be to deny him the humanity that he clearly relished. Kennedy's involvement in the drowning death of a young campaign aide named Mary Jo Kopechne in the summer of 1969 effectively short-circuited his burgeoning presidential ambitions—he was married at the time—and left a cloud hanging over his career. His allies insist it was a terrible accident; his critics believe Kopechne's death was a window into Kennedy's soul.

Kennedy eventually did run for president, challenging President Jimmy Carter in the Democratic primary in 1979—a race that he was expected to win and didn't. The lasting memory of that campaign was Kennedy's inability to answer the simple question of why he was running for president. Asked that question by CBS News's Roger Mudd, Kennedy hemmed and hawed for critical seconds before delivering a rambling answer that led people to question whether he had put any amount of serious thought behind what he would do if elected.

Following that defeat, Kennedy could well have walked away from politics. But instead, he stayed in the Senate and continued to work—demonstrating the dogged persistence that earns him a place in The Fix Political Hall of Fame. Kennedy eventually won nine elections to the Senate—and during the forty-six years he spent in the world's greatest deliberative body he helped author a series of major pieces of legislation including the Family and Medical Leave Act and No Child Left Behind, a piece of education reform legislation on which he worked with then president George W. Bush.

Kennedy's death in 2009 was not a surprise—he had been diagnosed with brain cancer the year before—but the outpouring of emotion for a man who had soldiered on through circumstances (both of his own doing and tragedies that seemed to find him and his family) that would have crushed less persistent souls was remarkable.

Kennedy's ability to be knocked down, get up, and move forward is virtually unequaled in modern politics. And that's why he's a Hall of Famer.

## JOHN McCAIN

The Arizona senator's life—both in and out of politics—has been defined by his ability to survive and, often, thrive.

The wild child of a major military family—he brags that he finished fifth from the bottom of his class at the U.S. Naval Academy—his life changed forever when he was shot down over Vietnam in October 1967. He spent the next five and a half years as a prisoner of war, an experience from which he emerged broken in body but resolute of mind—and as something close to a national hero. (The story of McCain turning down the opportunity for early release—he was regarded as a high-profile prisoner because his father was a navy admiral—quickly became the stuff of legend.)

Less than ten years later, McCain moved to Arizona—where he had never lived before—and, taking advantage of his personal story and the wealth of his father-in-law (McCain and his first wife officially divorced in April 1980 and he married Cindy Helmsley five weeks later), McCain won a House seat in the 1982 election.

He spent just two terms in the House before running for the Senate in 1986 for the seat being vacated by Senator Barry Goldwater, himself a major national figure who had run for and badly lost a presidential campaign in 1964. McCain cruised to a 60 percent to 40 percent victory over Richard Kimball—not the Fugitive—in the fall.

Once he got to the Senate, McCain came into full flower in a career defined by both his willingness to put himself in the middle of virtually every major bipartisan effort and his legendarily volcanic temper.

McCain's pet issue for years was the reform of the way campaigns are financed, and the passage of a law in the early 2000s that fundamentally altered how money flowed through the political system was a major accomplishment and a testament to McCain's legislative abilities. His involvement in the so-called Gang of 14—a group of centrist legislators from both parties aimed at avoiding a showdown over judicial confirmations—drew him praise among the media smart set but made him enemies among many conservatives. (More on that shortly.)

While McCain was well regarded in the Senate, when he announced in 1999 that he was planning to run for the Republican presidential nomination, he was not regarded as a top-tier contender. That honor fell to Texas governor George W. Bush, who had all the money, political support, and organization that McCain lacked.

It was in that campaign, however, that McCain turned himself into a major national figure. That ascent focused on a bus—oddly enough. The "Straight Talk Express" became an embodiment of McCain himself—freewheeling, old school, and appealing. McCain and his senior advisers would lounge in the back of the bus as he went from campaign stop to campaign stop—fielding any and every question that the press could throw at him. The contrast between McCain's ask-me-anything approach and Bush's buttoned-up campaign was striking. McCain became a cult figure—particularly in New Hampshire, where he crushed Bush by eighteen points.

That victory was relatively short-lived, however, as Bush famously/infamously savaged McCain in South Carolina—personally and politically—winning that state and effectively ending the nomination fight. That loss plunged McCain into a bit of a political wilderness as he clearly struggled with supporting Bush in the general election or staying within a party that had ganged up on him at the moment of his greatest possible triumph.

But McCain dug deep and, deciding he wanted to run for

president again, threw his full support behind Bush's 2004 reelection bid—emerging as one of the campaign's best surrogates. That effort paid off in 2008 as McCain—despite a series of peaks and valleys that left his campaign nearly broke in the summer of 2007—won the GOP nomination the second time around.

Again, though, McCain was thwarted in his ultimate goal—running into the electoral buzz saw that was then Illinois senator Barack Obama. While the dynamics of the 2008 election—Bush fatigue among other things—made it very unlikely that McCain could have won under any circumstances, his lack of interest in or knowledge about the economy badly hamstrung him. (His pronouncement that the "fundamentals of the economy are strong" in the middle of the 2008 economic crisis effectively doomed any chance he had.)

Rather than retire from the Senate when his term came up again in 2010, McCain soldiered on—remaking himself from a pragmatic moderate into a consistent conservative in order to beat back a challenge from his ideological right. That move won him the election but lost him the respect of many of the same chattering-class types who had fallen in love with him during his 2000 presidential campaign. McCain seemed not to care—content that he had, again, survived.

For having the best survival instincts in modern American politics, McCain is a first-ballot Fix Political Hall of Famer.

## NANCY PELOSI

Even before Pelosi was elected as the first female Speaker of the House in early 2007, she warranted consideration as a first-ballot Hall of Famer. Her political career, which began in the late 1970s, in many ways follows the arc of the Democratic Party over the past three decades.

Elected in a 1987 special election to a San Francisco–area House district, Pelosi joined a Democratic Party at the height of its power in the House. Democrats had held the House since the mid-1950s, and no one—including most Republicans—could imagine that changing, well, ever. Pelosi quickly was tagged for stardom by the likes of California representative George Miller and then New York representative Chuck Schumer. (She had politics in her blood; her father, Tommy D'Alessandro, was the mayor of Baltimore and a U.S. House member.)

Pelosi's fund-raising prowess and telegenic good looks gave her a seat at the table as Democrats governed with near-unchecked authority during the late 1980s and early 1990s. But, while Pelosi was close to the powerful, she didn't serve in an official leadership capacity, which preserved her political future when Democrats lost their House majority in the 1994 election. Cast into the minority, Pelosi was one of the key figures in leading her party back. That march began in earnest when she served on the House Ethics panel that investigated Speaker Newt Gingrich regarding his dealings with nonprofit groups that he used to advance his political agenda.

Pelosi's perch on Ethics raised her profile and gave her a foothold to make an official bid for leadership, which she did in 2001 when she was elected as House minority whip—the first woman to hold that position. Pelosi promptly bucked leadership—and established herself as the leading voice of liberal Democrats in the House—when she voted against the 2002 use-of-force resolution against Iraq. By 2003, she was elected minority leader.

Over the next three years, Pelosi built a political and fund-raising operation aimed at a single thing: winning back control of the House. She traveled the country in a relentless pursuit of campaign cash and installed Rahm Emanuel, the Democratic Party's best strategist, at the head of its campaign committee. The 2006 election turned out to be a perfect storm for Pelosi's ambitions; fatigue with President Bush coupled with a series of Republican scandals that culminated in Representative Mark Foley's inappropriate texting with House pages led to a national wave that crashed down on the GOP, gave Democrats the House majority, and made Pelosi a major historical figure as the first woman to serve in the top job in the U.S. House.

Surrounded by her children and grandchildren, Pelosi was sworn in as Speaker on January 6, 2007. "For our daughters and grand-daughters, today we have broken the marble ceiling," she said. "For our daughters and our granddaughters, the sky is the limit, anything is possible for them."

The 2008 election gave Pelosi not only more Democrats in the House but a Democrat in the White House—developments that seemed to lay the groundwork for long-term Democratic domi-nance but were, ultimately, the first signs of major problems brew-ing for the party. Pelosi went to work instituting President Obama's agenda—most notably health care and the economic stimulus pack-age. Meanwhile, Republicans were hard at work turning Pelosi into a Democratic demon—taking advantage of her heightened profile to cast her as a San Francisco liberal fundamentally out of step with the average voter in the country.

By the time the 2010 election rolled around, Republicans had suc-ceeded in the demonization of Pelosi. She was featured in hundreds of ads run by Republican candidates and conservative groups—all of which sought to use her negative image as an anchor around the legs of aspiring Democratic candidates, many of whom did everything they could to distance themselves from Pelosi.

When Democrats lost sixty-three seats and their House majority in November 2010, everyone—including me—expected Pelosi to step aside. After all, who would want to serve as the House minority leader after spending four years as the chamber's Speaker? (There is nothing—I repeat, nothing—worse than being in the House minor-ity. You are constantly being rolled by the majority. To the extent you score victories, they are on rinky-dink procedural things that the gen-eral public doesn't know or care about.)

Pelosi, as it turned out, had other plans. Resisting calls from some within the Democratic House caucus for her to step aside so that the party could move on, Pelosi announced her candidacy for minority leader and easily won the post thanks to her continued support from the liberal end of the party. Her reasons are her own, but, as best as I could report out, she desperately wanted to win the House back and didn't see anyone waiting in the wings who could raise the money to make it happen.

Pelosi will be seventy-two years old when voters vote this November. Her party needs twenty-five seats to win back the majority, and most independent analysts think it's a long shot. If Democrats make gains but don't win back the majority, does Pelosi spend another two years traveling the country in search of ever more campaign cash and candidates who can win? Or does she walk away?

Regardless of what happens in November, Pelosi is, without question, the most influential House member in the past twenty-five years. And for that, she gets a spot in our Political Hall of Fame.

# BUILDING THE PERFECT THIRD-PARTY PRESIDENTIAL CANDIDATE

Independents are the new "it" girl of American politics. As the two parties in Washington—and around the country—continue to grow further apart in their ideological views, the middle is being occupied more and more by people who call themselves unaffiliated voters.

A *USA Today* study released in late 2011 showed that the two major American political parties had shed 2.5 million voters since the 2008 election. In the twenty-eight states that register voters by party, Democratic registration has shrunk in twenty-five of them, while Republican registration has receded in twenty-one. The *USA Today* survey found even starker registration losses in six states—Colorado,

Florida, Iowa, Nevada, New Hampshire, and Pennsylvania—likely to be closely contested by the two parties this fall; Democratic registration dropped in those six states by 800,000 while Republican registration dipped by 350,000. Those affiliated as independents rose by 350,000 in those six states.

Polling bears that movement out. Gallup found that 40 percent of all Americans identified themselves as independents in 2011, the highest that number has been in the history of the poll. Thirty-one percent of respondents described themselves as Democrats while 27 percent said they were Republicans. "If national conditions and the political environment do not change appreciably over the course of this year, independent identification—even if it declines—will probably remain on the higher end of what Gallup has measured historically," wrote Gallup's Jeff Jones in a memo documenting the results.

All of those numbers point to one obvious political reality: the country is as ready as it ever has been for the emergence of another party in the political process. And there are a number of groups organizing to make that happen in the 2012 election.

That movement is led by Americans Elect, an organization composed of Democratic and Republican political operatives that worked to gain ballot access for a third-party candidacy. By this spring, Americans Elect had gained a spot for a third-party candidate on the ballots of twenty-five states, including such large ones as California and Florida. Given that ballot access is always the biggest problem for anyone wanting to run outside of the two-party system—it's a state-by-state process that often requires painstaking (and costly) signature collection—the bottom-up approach taken by Americans Elect reflects one of the most nuanced approaches to building a third party that I've seen in decades.

And yet, by the end of May, Americans Elect had failed to field a candidate and admitted defeat. (Talk about going out with a whimper.) The failure of Americans Elect is the latest evidence that a third-party movement simply will not happen—maybe ever. Here are three reasons why.

# 1. MOST PEOPLE AREN'T REALLY INDEPENDENTS

Given the eye-rolling partisanship that exists on both the extreme right and the extreme left, it's become cool to declare yourself a political free agent. Most people like to think of themselves as someone who makes a reasoned assessment issue by issue rather than someone who reflexively sides with whatever partisan viewpoint one party puts forward.

That's all well and good. But it's not real political life. The truth of politics—a truth proven in focus groups and polling conducted over the past decade—is that most independents tend to side with one party or the other the vast majority of the time. That is, they think of themselves as free agents—able to choose whichever side they agree with more often in a given election—but they are actually partisans, almost always siding with the same side, in disguise.

A *Washington Post*/Kaiser/Harvard poll conducted in 2007 broke independents into five distinct groups, with two of those subcategories being "closet" partisans on the right and left. Those "disguised partisans generally walk and talk like Democrats or Republicans—sometimes with even more passion," wrote Dan Balz and Jon Cohen in the *Washington Post*. "They reject party labels but usually back one side or the other." Larry Parker, who directs a day care center in Vermont, is indicative of these "closet" partisans. "I generally don't support Republicans," Parker told Balz and Cohen. "I definitely support Democrats the majority of the time. I'm an independent because I like to keep an open mind."

Being independent-minded and being politically independent, of course, are two very different things. And the reality is that large swaths of people who call themselves independents are simply using that term to distinguish themselves from what they believe to be the nonthinking predictability of partisans in the two parties. Identifying as an independent then is aspirational; it's more how they see themselves in their own mind's eye than how they actually act in a political context. (In my mind's eye, I have a deep voice like James Earl Jones, but somehow on TV that basso profundo turns into a high-pitched girlish timbre.) But aspiring to be an independent and actually being one are two very different things.

## 2. INDEPENDENTS ARE NOT A UNIFIED IDEOLOGICAL BLOC

The tendency in politics—and political reporting—is to oversimplify things. Hispanics are Democrats, evangelicals are Republicans, and so on and so forth.

Independents fall prey to this same sort of wrongheaded logic. Since they aren't affiliated with either party, they *must* all think similarly and agree on the reasons why they don't feel comfortable permanently or even semipermanently attaching themselves to one of the two major parties.

A Pew poll released in 2011 proved the fallacy of this assumption. Known as the Political Typology survey—Pew conducts this poll once every five or six years—it aims not just to sort out the percentages of people who call themselves Democrats, Republicans, or independents but also to drill down deeper into what common traits (if any) emerge from within these groups. And the Pew Political Typology survey makes clear that lumping all independents into a single political silo badly misses the mark.

"Independents have played a determinative role in the last three national elections," reads the memo Pew released to accompany the poll's results. "But the three groups in the center of the political typology have very little in common, aside from their avoidance of partisan labels."

Pew breaks down independents into three distinct subgroups: Libertarians, Post-Moderns, and Disaffecteds. (Naming these groups must be so much fun. Soccer moms! Defense dads!) Describing the three independent groups, the pollsters write:

> Libertarians and Post-Moderns are largely white, well-educated and affluent. They also share a relatively secular outlook on some social issues, including homosexuality and abortion. But Republican-oriented Libertarians are far more critical of government, less supportive of environmental regulations, and more supportive of business than are Post-Moderns, most of whom lean Democratic. Disaffecteds, the other main group of independents, are financially stressed and cynical about politics. Most lean to the Republican Party, though they differ from the core Republican groups in their support for increased government aid to the poor.

Just 19 percent of Post-Moderns consider themselves conservatives, while 42 percent of Disaffecteds and 53 percent of Libertarians said the same. Sixty-one percent of Disaffecteds agreed with the sentiment that "government should do more to help the needy" while just 27 percent of Post-Moderns and just 10 percent of Libertarians said the same.

Given that data, it makes *no* sense to try to make broad assumptions about "which way the independent vote will go." The independent vote is a fallacy; the group of people who describe themselves as independents are simply not a monolithic voting bloc—or anything close to it.

## 3. THERE IS NO CANDIDATE

The simplest rule of politics is that you can't beat something with nothing. In other words, though a candidate may well be flawed, you can't beat him (or her) without a candidate of your own.

And there simply isn't any obvious third-party candidate waiting in the wings to capitalize on the dissatisfaction that is clearly coursing through the electorate. Let's go over the most mentioned options—and why they won't work.

## MICHAEL BLOOMBERG

Yes, the mayor of New York's personal wealth—he is a billionaire—and middle-of-the-road politics make him all the rage of the *Morning Joe* set. But consider this: Bloomberg is a single (and divorced) Jewish man from the Northeast who has been a leading voice on the need for more gun control laws on the books. In what swing state is that profile a winning one? Not any that I can think of. Add to that Bloomberg's lack of enthusiam about the drudgery entailed in running for president, and a bid doesn't look likely—or likely to succeed.

## JON HUNTSMAN

The former Utah governor is a Republican that Democrats love. While it's easy to diagnose his loss in the 2012 Republican presidential primary as evidence that he was simply too much of a centrist for the GOP and, hence, would make an ideal third-party candidate, the lack of lift for Huntsman's candidacy had as much to do with his lack of charisma as his lack of conservative bona fides. Huntsman looks good on paper, but he never could translate an impressive résumé into anything more than that on the campaign trail. And if he couldn't do that in a Republican primary, why would he be able to pull off that trick in a general election where he would be drowned out by the messaging and money of the two major party candidates?

## RON PAUL

The Texas congressman, who ran for president as a Libertarian in 1988, is without question the most viable third-party candidate of this trio. But he's far from the sort of sensible centrist that groups like Americans

Elect are aiming to recruit to the process. Paul has a following—most national polls give him 12 to 18 percent in a three-way matchup with President Obama and Mitt Romney—but it's a following built on his Libertarian ideals of ending the Federal Reserve, returning to the gold standard, and adopting a noninterventionist—some would say isolationist—approach to foreign policy. Paul might make the biggest impact as a third-party candidate, but it certainly wouldn't be in the way most advocates of a new party envision it being born.

There is always the possibility that someone could appear out of nowhere—Ross Perot–style—and shake up the race. That would almost certainly have to be a very rich individual who could fund his/her own campaign ads. While there are plenty of rich business-men and -women in the country, most of them prefer to stay out of elected office and keep their money. Politics is, frankly, a hell of a lot harder than it looks, and the road to office is littered with wealthy individuals who thought their successes in the private sector would translate into electoral success. The most recent, though far from the only, example is former eBay CEO Meg Whitman, who spent $107 million, almost all of it her own money, on a 2010 bid for governor of California. For all that money, Whitman got scads of negative press and a resounding loss at the hands of the current governor, Jerry Brown.

Since there isn't a perfect third-party candidate for 2012, I decided to build one—$6 million man/woman style. So come into The Fix laboratory with me as I construct the perfect third-party candidate.

## The looks . . . of JON HUNTSMAN: The former Utah governor just looks like a president. He's got perfectly coiffed gray hair. He's tan but not too tan. He's not short but neither is he impos-ingly tall. He can pull off a business suit as well as blue jeans and cowboy boots—a rare thing in American politics.

**The issues . . . of ROSS PEROT:** Go back and watch the 1992 presidential debates. Or the long infomercials that Perot paid for during that campaign. What you'll see is a terrific message and the wrong messenger. Everything that Perot was talking about twenty years ago—runaway debt, politicians not willing to make hard decisions—is true tenfold now. The problem was that Perot got in the way of his own message. His strong southern accent, his (lack of) size, and his erratic (at times) behavior all distracted from the fact that he was right when it came to matters of debt and spending.

**The money of . . . MICHAEL BLOOMBERG:** Bloomberg is a billionaire, but it's how he made it that makes him perfect to run as an independent. He didn't manage a hedge fund or inherit it from his parents. He made it by building a massive media company. In the eyes of most—though not all—voters, that's about the cleanest (and best) way you can become a very rich man these days. Side benefit: Bloomberg literally owns a not-insignificant portion of the media. Not that it would influence how he's covered, but still . . .

**The personality of . . . LINDSAY GRAHAM:** The South Carolina senator is an underrated political talent. He's one of the few politicians who get politics, get policy, and get how policy and politics work together. And Graham's personality—particularly on television—is just the sort of thing you want in an independent politician. He appears to be candid most of the time and has a down-homey-ness (not a real word) that humanizes him. Graham can be—and often is—funny, an underrated trait among politicians.

**The integrity of . . . TOM COBURN:** Coburn, a senator from Oklahoma, and President Obama agree on almost no issue. Coburn is among the most conservative members of the Senate, while Obama, during his brief time there, was among the most liberal. But the two men get along. Why? Because Coburn actually believes what he says. Yes, he's conservative on most issues but he's also bucked his party on spending issues—particularly earmarking. Coburn isn't afraid to stand against the shibboleths of both parties. And that's exactly what you need in a third-party candidate.

# KIRSTEN GILLIBRAND: THE NEXT HILLARY?

When Hillary Clinton ended her presidential campaign on June 8, 2008, she uttered these now famous words: "Although we weren't able to shatter that highest, hardest glass ceiling this time, thanks to you, it's got about eighteen million cracks in it. And the light is shining through like never before, filling us all with the hope and the sure knowledge that the path will be a little easier next time."

While the line drew wild applause from the crowd who had gathered at the National Building Museum to see Clinton formally call it quits, a look behind the rhetorical curtain didn't provide much optimism for those hoping to see a female president in their lifetimes.

Clinton was one of sixteen women in the Senate at the time; only one—North Carolina Republican senator Elizabeth Dole—had run for president before. (None have run since.) There were eight women governors; with the exception of Alaska's own Sarah Palin none of them had appeared before, or has since, on a national ticket.

While women had made rapid progress in terms of expanding their ranks in Congress—and at the gubernatorial level—there were very few females in the political pipeline who were regarded as national candidate material. Clinton had been the great female hope for as long as anyone could remember. From her pre-Bill days—she appeared in *Life* magazine after delivering the commencement address at Wellesley—through her time as first lady and, especially, once she was elected to the Senate in 2000, there was little doubt in the mind of anyone—male or female—that if a woman was going to be elected president, Hillary was the one.

Then she lost. At that moment, few people would have picked Kirsten Gillibrand as the person who might pick up the presidential standard that Clinton put down that day. But those people don't know Gillibrand's history very well. Gillibrand traces her interest (and success) in politics to three women. "Women matter and they often can put partisan politics aside," said Gillibrand. "They are better at getting things done."

The first woman Gillibrand credits with her success is her grandmother, Dorothea "Polly" Noonan, who began as a secretary in the New York state legislature at age twenty and grew to be a major force in Albany as a voice for women running for office. She was a close confidante of Albany mayor Erastus Corning and an associate of Daniel O'Connell, the man who controlled the Albany Democratic political machine for five decades (!) beginning in the 1920s. Of that trio, former New York governor Mario Cuomo told the *New York Times* in 2009 that "Dan O'Connell was the nominal leader. Corning was the de facto leader. Polly was the leader."

Gillibrand called her grandmother a "larger-than-life" figure who was a "hardball player to the core." Sitting in her Senate office, she recounts with a smile the days when she would be sitting in some

Democrat's campaign headquarters stuffing envelopes or, as often happened, putting bumper stickers on cars. (Gillibrand says that her grandmother used to deploy her and her cousins to put bumper stickers supporting her candidate over the bumper stickers supporting their opponents. After all, who could get mad at a kid for a little campaign dirty trick?)

The second person Gillibrand credits with her rise is her mother, Polly Rutnik, a lawyer who was one of only three women in her law school class at Suffolk University. ("Judges would call her 'little lady,' " recalls Gillibrand.) Gillibrand said that in an age when most of her friends' mothers chose to stay at home, her mom "decided to have a career" and, in so doing, became a "role model" for her and her circle of friends. Gillibrand proudly notes that of her six closest high school friends, five of them—including herself—went on to become lawyers.

And the third is Hillary Clinton. As a young lawyer in New York City in 1995, Gillibrand heard a speech that Clinton, then the first lady, gave in China making the case that "human rights are women's rights—and women's rights are human rights." Said Gillibrand of that speech: "I felt inside that I wasn't doing enough. Why was I not at that convention in Beijing?" Gillibrand's first step was to get involved with the Women's Leadership Forum, a group designed to train women for positions of, well, leadership in and out of public life. (Gillibrand said that it cost her $1,000 to join WLF, the largest check she had ever written—except for rent in New York—in her life.) Clinton was deeply involved in WLF and provided the impetus not only for Gillibrand to raise money for those in office but also to actually get involved herself. "She gave a speech that spoke to me," said Gillibrand. "She said that if you don't participate, you leave it to those who do and you may not like what they do. She's so right." Clinton, says Gillibrand, made her believe that women could and should run for office. ("I doubted myself," she acknowledged. "How could I run for office? How could I be so bold? How could I be so arrogant?")

It was also through WLF that Gillibrand found a foothold in politics. After being turned down by the U.S. attorney's office as well as by the Ford Foundation and the Carnegie Endowment—"I didn't even get an interview," she said—Gillibrand decided to approach Andrew Cuomo, then the secretary of housing and urban development, after a speech he gave to WLF. Cuomo asked her if she was willing to move to Washington. She said yes, despite being up for partner at her law firm. Cuomo hired her as special counsel for the final seven months before the 2000 election, which, after Democrats lost, left Gillibrand without a job but with a major political bug.

She went back to work in corporate law but eventually moved to upstate New York—her father, Doug Rutnik, is a lobbyist and major force in state politics—to make a run for Congress in what looked like, at the time, a quixotic bid against Representative John Sweeney (R). Her candidacy became far less of a long shot as the race wore on, however, and Sweeney revealed himself to be a very flawed candidate (and person). First came pictures of a decidedly inebriated Sweeney at a fraternity party at Union College at Schenectady. Then came reports, just days before the election, that Sweeney's wife had called the police because the congressman was "knocking her around." Sweeney insisted the allegations were overstated and blamed Gillibrand for making them public. It didn't matter. Gillibrand won. And most people assumed that's where Gillibrand's political career would take her—a nice, steady life.

Enter David Paterson, the embattled governor tasked with picking a replacement for Clinton, who was named secretary of state by President Obama in late 2008. Paterson's search, which took on a soap operatic quality, included the likes of Andrew Cuomo, who took himself out of contention, and Caroline Kennedy, the daughter of the former president, whose unsteady public presence disqualified her as a choice. Gillibrand was the last person left standing and wound up being Paterson's pick after a remarkably public process. Gillibrand, in a bow to her relative anonymity for most New Yorkers, had this to say when she was picked: "For many in New York State, this is the first time you've heard my name, and you don't know much about me. Over the next two years, you will get to know me. And, more importantly, I will get to know you." (So unknown was Gillibrand that the Associated Press ran a pronouncer—JILL-ih-brand—with the story announcing her appointment.)

Though Paterson touted her credentials as a moderate—she voted against several gun control measures in the House—Gillibrand quickly moved to the ideological left, recognizing the political leanings of the Empire State and of her future on the national political stage. (Gillibrand was the tenth most liberal senator, according to the 2010 vote ratings conducted by *National Journal* magazine—to the left of the likes of Minnesota senator Al Franken, for example.) She has also developed an issue portfolio sure to appeal to liberal Democrats; Gillibrand, for example, was leading agitator for the repeal of the "Don't Ask, Don't Tell" policy regarding gays in the military. (Gillibrand was the first person in public life to shine a light on the dismissal of Lieutenant Dan Choi for being gay and was a major force for Senate hearings on the idea of repeal.) In an e-mail sent to her supporters, Gillibrand sought to lay claim to the credit for the repeal, which passed the Senate in late 2010: "It's been a long, hard road, and I couldn't have done it without your support," she wrote.

Gillibrand's pet issue, however, is transparency. She was the first member of Congress to put her official schedule online—including her meetings with lobbyists—and is one of only ten senators who files her fund-raising reports electronically with the Federal Election Commission. (In a bit of ridiculous arcana, senators still file paper reports detailing their contributions and expenditures to the secretary of the Senate. They are then uploaded—page by page—to the Internet, a laborious process that can delay access to the information for weeks.)

"Sunlight is the most effective disinfectant," she explained. "If I am being lobbied by Group A, I want Group B to know. I thought our democracy would work better if people knew who I was taking meetings with." A focus on transparency—cleaning up a government that most people believe doesn't serve their interests—is a message that could well be a foundational building block of a presidential platform for Gillibrand.

Gillibrand's aides insist neither she nor they discuss—publicly or privately—the possibility of her running for president in 2016. But the facts are these: the most oft-mentioned candidates—Cuomo, Maryland governor Martin O'Malley, Virginia senator Mark Warner—are all middle-aged, white males. And it's hard to overestimate how big an advantage being a woman in a Democratic presidential primary field full of men actually is. Fifty-seven percent of the participants in the 2008 Iowa Democratic presidential caucuses and New Hampshire primary were women; Clinton lost the female vote to Obama in Iowa but won it by double digits in New Hampshire. (Clinton's problem was not that she was a woman but that she was running against an African American candidate who more successfully consolidated that competing pillar of the Democratic base.)

There is a coveted slot then in any Democratic primary but particularly a presidential primary for a woman. And Gillibrand may be the woman best positioned—and most willing—to take the leap. The only other obvious person—whose politics might line up with a Democratic primary electorate—is Minnesota's Amy Klobuchar, who seems to have little interest in national office. The other Democratic women in the Senate are either too old (Dianne Feinstein, Barbara Mikulski) or too moderate (Claire McCaskill, Mary Landrieu) to qualify as potentially serious contenders. Among the nation's Democratic female governors, the presidential picks are decidedly thin too. There are only two women governors at the moment—Christine Gregoire in Washington State and Bev Perdue in North Carolina. Gregoire could run but has made no move toward doing so. Perdue was so unpopular in her home state that she decided not to seek a second term in November.

That leaves the likes of Gillibrand who is (a) a woman, (b) a (converted) liberal, (c) a fund-raising dynamo, and (d) from a large state with major influence in Democratic Party politics.

To (c): since 2007, Gillibrand has raised more than $23 million—a massive sum that allowed her to avoid a serious challenge in either her 2010 race (a special election to allow her to serve out the remaining two years of Clinton's term) or her 2012 bid for a full six-year term. Fund-raising is the first bar that any presidential candidate needs to show he/she can clear. Without the ability to raise between $10 and $20 million—and likely much, much more—in the year before the Iowa caucuses and New Hampshire primary, it's difficult for a candidate to be taken seriously. (Amazing but true.) Of the women contemplating—or mentioned as contemplating—presidential bids for Democrats in 2016, only Gillibrand has raised that amount of money before. And having done it before means she can—theoretically—do it again.

What all of the above tells me is that if Gillibrand wants to run for president, she and those close to her can make a solid case internally that she would at least have a chance at running a serious campaign. Of course there are major unanswered questions that could make all of Gillibrand's presidential aspirations—if she, as I strongly suspect she does, has them—moot.

Gillibrand remains an almost entirely unproven candidate on the national stage. Yes, she has prospered—to date—in the confrontational world of the New York media, but she hasn't undergone the full combing-through of her personal and political life that happens to every person who runs for president. Gillibrand's position switches—conservative to liberal—from her time in the House to her time in the Senate would be fodder for her opponents (I can already imagine some sort of "wolf in sheep's clothing" ad) as would her bare-knuckled approach to politics. She would also likely have to weather questions about whether she had enough (or the right) experience to serve as the Democratic standard-bearer. In 2016, she will have spent less than a decade in the Senate after serving in the House for a single full term.

Politics, of course, is about taking chances. Leaping even (or especially) when the outcome is murky is the hallmark of all great politicians. There are no sure things in politics; just ask Hillary Clinton. Gillibrand seems to understand intuitively the need to take risks, a trait she credits—not surprisingly—to her grandmother. "Never be afraid of trying," Gillibrand recalls her grandmother telling her. "The fight is worth the fight." If she runs for president in 2016, that could well be Gillibrand's campaign slogan.

# THE FOUR-STAR POLITICAL GENERAL, RETIRED (SORT OF)

Ask Mike Murphy what his role is in the Republican Party and he reaches for a military metaphor. "I am like an old retired four-star general," says Murphy. "I get to say what I want and a few of the younger officers tend to listen to me."

While the whole politics-as-warfare metaphor is pretty played out, Murphy's comparison is apt. After three decades spent in the trenches of Republican campaign politics serving as a media consultant and strategist, Murphy is now semiretired—living in California and, oddly for a Republican, pursuing a writing career in Hollywood. "I made a lot of money, I had a big reputation . . . I was pretty much the guy to get in blue state governors' races," he says somewhat tongue-in-cheek when asked to explain his switch from politics to entertainment. "I was getting a little bored with it."

And for good reason. Murphy opened his own consulting business—along with fellow media svengali Alex Castellanos—at age twenty. He started working in politics in 1981 as an intern for NCPAC, a political organization long affiliated with Republican consulting godfathers Arthur Finkelstein and Terry Dolan. By 1982, Murphy had, by his own admission, "stopped showing up at college"—he was in the School of Foreign Service at Georgetown University—and had gone into business with Castellanos. For the next eight years, Murphy and Castellanos worked hand in hand building their business; they landed Georgia senator Mack Mattingly's reelection race in 1986 (he lost) but helped guide Steve Symms, an Idaho Republican, to a second term that same year.

Murphy and Castellanos parted ways in 1989—Murphy describes the split as "incredibly amicable"—and Murphy started his own firm. He proceeded to go on an enviable winning streak in the 1990s, helping elect governors in New Jersey (Christine Todd Whitman), Michigan (John Engler), Florida (Jeb Bush), Wisconsin (Tommy Thompson), and Massachusetts (Mitt Romney). (There were losses mixed in there too; Murphy did Lamar Alexander's 1996 presidential bid, for one.) "The way I see myself is that I have about the best record in blue and purple state victories in the party over the last twenty years," said Murphy.

Then Murphy met Arnold Schwarzenegger, who was running in the California gubernatorial recall election in 2003. Schwarzenegger, an action star turned Republican activist, gave Murphy entrée into a whole new world—entertainment—that intrigued him. After Schwarzenegger won, Murphy, who was living in California by that time, decided to forsake politics for a career in show business. He wrote for comedian Dennis Miller, a rare Republican in Hollywood. He sold a pilot to HBO. And, perhaps most remarkably for a man who had spent the past two decades helping elect Republicans to office, he marched in the 2007 Writers Guild strike. ("I am in two unions," joked Murphy.)

Of course, like all "retired" political consultants, Murphy is never really out of the game. In 2010, he served as the chief strategist for former eBay executive Meg Whitman's failed California gubernatorial bid—a race she spent $107 million of her own money on but still wound up losing convincingly to septuagenarian Jerry Brown. Murphy insisted that despite that dalliance with Whitman, he remains done (or close to it) with political campaigns.

But simply because he no longer needs to work in campaigns doesn't mean Murphy has cured himself of the political bug. And, in that, Murphy sees himself in direct competition with Karl Rove, a long-time political rival. "There are two churches in the party," explains Murphy. "How do you grab independents and swing voters versus how do you increase turnout in your crowd." Murphy is the de facto pastor in that first church; Rove runs the second one.

The 2000 primary fight between Texas governor George W. Bush and Arizona senator John McCain was, to those in the know, a proxy fight between those two churches and the two men who led them. Rove had long groomed Bush for national office—Rove got his start in politics as a direct-mail consultant in the Lone Star State—while Murphy was one of the central members of the McCain campaign.

The campaigns themselves reflected the two strategists at their hearts. Bush ran a tight ship built around discipline, money, and organization. Reporters were granted very limited access to the candidate—if they were lucky. McCain, on the other hand, had the Straight Talk Express, the political equivalent of a Volkswagen bus, in which the candidate, Murphy, and a few other aides toured the country. Reporters were invited to hang out for as long as they liked, asking McCain questions until they ran out of questions to ask. Rove was almost always in a suit and tie. Murphy wore wrinkled khakis and had hipster glasses and a wild bit of longish hair on his balding pate. Bush/Rove was IBM; McCain/Murphy was Apple. IBM won. While McCain and his band of political rogues put a major scare into the Bush world when the Arizona senator shocked the Texas governor with a win in New Hampshire, the Bush machine eventually ground down the upstart's campaign. That defeat sent lots of Team McCain into the political wilderness. "A lot of guys in that world have left politics," said Murphy. "All of the tribal allegiances with Bush in 2000 were Karl's guys."

If 2000 was a major moment for Rove, 2004 was his crowning achievement. While most campaigns and candidates spent the vast majority of their time and money trying to convince independent voters to side with them, Rove and the senior campaign team put equal—if not greater—emphasis on identifying and turning out the GOP base. "Nobody had ever approached an election that I've looked at over the last fifty years, where base motivation was as important as swing, which is how we approached it," explained Bush pollster Matthew Dowd. "Our goal was to say that we wanted the same number of Republicans on election day as Democrats, and if we saw that we had the same number of people that said they were Republicans on election day as Democrats, we were going to win the election, no matter what happened among the small group of persuadable voters."

Bush's victory was, to Rove and his acolytes, a validation of the base strategy. It had, after all, helped reelect an unpopular president who appeared dead in the political water a year before the election. But, for Murphy, Bush's victory taught the Republican political class the wrong lessons. Rove's approach is a "beautiful way to win Oklahoma but you lose Michigan and Wisconsin with it," according to Murphy. That is, focusing on the base is a terrific strategy in states where there is a large GOP base on which to focus but a far less smart approach in swing states or in places where Democrats outnumber Republicans. "Bad skills at a bad college have weakened the operatives," insists Murphy. "We are very short on strategists and very long on tacticians."

Murphy believes that the strategist shortage, when coupled with the fact that the party is "ignoring demographics" in its policies toward the Hispanic community, represent the two major challenges for the GOP heading into November and beyond. "We have to modernize conservatism to fit the present time," insisted Murphy. "We need to be accepting of the multicultural reality of it." The question is whether Murphy will play an active role in that debate or the passive one he has assumed since McCain came up short more than a decade ago. Murphy's career since then—with one foot in Hollywood but the other still firmly planted in the political world (he regularly appears on NBC's Sunday talk show *Meet the Press*)—is reflective of the internal tension he feels: drawn to politics but never wanting to be just another voice in the crowd. "My dread was that I would have to do campaigns for money," he said.

But walking away from politics doesn't seem to be in his blood. Murphy jokes—continuing the retired general metaphor—that he sits at home wearing his "ill-fitting civilian clothes" and ruminating on what might have been and what still could be. It's hard to imagine him doing anything else.

# WHAT'S THE NEW, NEW THING?

Good politicians take what people are telling them—their hopes, concerns, etc.—and turn it into a winning message. Great politicians reach something inside you that you might not have even known was there. They get you to believe in something, something bigger than you, your family, and your friends. They make you think things can be different, better. They capture the cultural zeitgeist in a word, a phrase, a speech, or an entire campaign. That's what differentiates the goods from the greats.

Voters want to feel that elections are about *big* things, not small ones. They see national elections as a chance to change, stop, or reshape the direction the country is currently headed. They tend to see their vote as an affirmation or a rejection of the big ideas that they believe the president has. (Of course, the big ideas that people think the president has and the actual big ideas he has—or doesn't have—are often very different.) Politicians who play to that desire for the next *big* thing—whether it's a candidate, an idea, or something else—tend to win. Those who go small often, though not always, come up short.

Take Ronald Reagan, whose sunny optimism in the midst of major political and policy challenges at home and abroad gave people a reason to hope after four years of Jimmy Carter telling them that things were slowly but surely getting worse in the country—and that the time had come to simply accept our new reality. "I will not stand by and watch this great country destroy itself under mediocre leadership that drifts from one crisis to the next, eroding our national will and purpose," Reagan said in a speech in June 1980. "The time is now, my fellow Americans, to recapture our destiny, to take it into our own hands."

Remember, this was a country still trying to make peace with the war in Vietnam, reeling from Watergate (still), a gas crisis, and the ongoing hostage situation in Iran. It hadn't been a very good past decade for America. There was a sense of creeping vulnerability that most Americans had never felt before. Reagan seemed to understand that worry intuitively, and much of his 1980 campaign and, frankly, his eight years in the White House was aimed at telling America that everything was going to be all right. Reagan grasped far better than Carter or any other politician in either party that assurance and optimism were the key words of the 1980s political culture. He was the grandfatherly figure who made us believe that everything was going to be all right (accidental Naughty by Nature reference!).

Fast-forward twenty-eight years to the 2008 election of Barack Obama. The country had just slogged through eight years of President George W. Bush—two terms that included the terrorist attacks of September 11, 2001, the wars in Iraq and Afghanistan, and, at the end, a vast, global financial collapse.

In the middle of those eight years, a little-known Illinois state senator named Barack Obama got elected to the U.S. Senate. And by the time 2008 rolled around, it became clear that Obama had mastered the zeitgeist of this age better than Hillary Clinton, John McCain, Rudy Giuliani, or anyone else running for president of the United States.

Obama's basic message of "hope and change" wasn't drastically different from what Reagan ran on in 1980. But where Reagan ran on the idea that America retained its pole position on the world stage, Obama's message centered on the sentiment that politics and politicians no longer effectively served those who elected them. The blame for that disconnect, according to Obama, was rightly placed at the feet of partisanship and politicians who worked to divide the country for their own selfish gains. "I don't want to pit Red America against Blue America," Obama said frequently on the campaign trail. "I want to be president of the United States of America."

What Obama understood was that the American public had grown sick and tired of politics as usual. They hated both parties. They felt like the two sides were nominating the same people—products of a corrupt party establishment—over and over again, just like how pro sports teams tend to recycle the same coaches they fired three years ago when looking for a new coach. Obama promised something different—in the way he looked, in his résumé, in the way he talked. He was black. He had only served in the U.S. Senate for two years before he decided to run for president. He didn't talk in bite-size, quotable chunks but in long, flowing prose. Everything about him screamed "CHANGE." It was easy for people to believe that—finally—they had found someone who could break the old partisan logjams in Washington and make the government run the way they always thought it might be capable of.

Voting for Obama then became a vote not just for a different candidate and party in the White House but also for a different kind of politics entirely. Obama won not because of issues—can you remember a single "issue" he ran on other than to make the economy better?—but on a sense that he embodied the change people were looking for. Obama's ability to capture the zeitgeist of the moment is why he was able to carry states like Indiana, North Carolina, and Virginia—states where no Democrat had won dating all the way back to 1976 or earlier. Democrats, independents, and even some Republicans voted for an idea (genuine change), not an issue set.

(It's also the reason why the blowback to Obama has been so strong in his first term in office. Many more conservative voters insist they were duped by Obama's promises and are resentful that they bought a bill of goods. In truth, however, that's not Obama's fault. He was the change vessel that voters poured *their* idea of "change" into. And—surprise, surprise—not everyone defines change the same way.)

All of which brings us to the 2012 election. What is it that's driving voters that Obama and Romney need to find a way to acknowledge and react to? I'll some it up in a single word: *anxiety*.

We are in an anxious time. The last four years have featured a nightly drumbeat of negative economic headlines—from the collapse (and bailout) of the financial industry in 2008 to the mortgage crisis to Bernie Madoff. Those doubts have been doubled (or more) by the collapse of any number of institutions that people have long relied on and, somewhere in their brains, believed would be around forever. Banks? Insolvent. Church? (Still) reeling from a sexual abuse scandal. Government? Increasingly clueless. National security? Tenuous. The onetime pillars of our political society have either fractured entirely or begun to show considerable wear and tear. Nothing feels solid anymore. The idea that we will figure things out no longer has the resonance that it once did.

That anxiety has, not surprisingly, affected our politics. We are jumpy and frenetic politically these days. Independent voters pinball between voting for Republicans and Democrats, hoping against hope for solutions that they secretly suspect neither party really has. Democrats were handed control of every lever of the federal government in 2008 only to see the House flip to Republicans in 2010—and with a very real chance that the Senate and White House will do the same this November. The American public is, at the moment, a chicken running around with its head cut off; it is scampering this way and that with no sense of direction or purpose.

That reality makes being a politician incredibly difficult. (It's already a really, really tough job.) Most politicians do best when they are able to give their voters what they want. But if voters don't know what that is, it puts politicians in a very tough spot. The burden rests on those running for office to—gulp—lead, to show the American public where we need to go and why. The president is the captain of the ship—bad metaphor alert!—and he (or she) needs to point in a direction and say: "Here's the direction we are heading. Not all of you may agree that it's the right direction. But get behind me and let's make sure we get there."

Obama has chosen a Reagan-like direction in which to try and lead the country. In his 2012 State of the Union speech, Obama repeatedly attempted to rekindle the "can-do" spirit that, he argued, defines Americans. "We can do this," he said at one point. "I know we can, because we've done it before. At the end of World War II, when another generation of heroes returned home from combat, they built the strongest economy and middle class the world has ever known." He also sought to tap back into the postpartisan sentiment that worked so well for him four years ago: "What's at stake aren't Democratic values or Republican values, but American values," said Obama.

The counterargument from Mitt Romney is that while Obama talks a good game on the exceptionalism of America and its people, his actions in office belie that belief. "He'd like to make us more like Europe, more like a European social welfare state," Romney regularly says when asked about Obama's approach to governance.

Unpack the Romney case against Obama and it amounts to this: Obama believes that government is the answer to the collective anxiety we as a country face. He doesn't believe individuals are capable of turning the country around. He doesn't believe in the free market. He doesn't believe in business and private industry as the engine of innovation and economic progress. Romney, on the other hand, believes in all of those things. He believes that the American people—when empowered to do so—can accomplish anything. Government needs to (mostly) get out of the way and let the inherent smarts and sensibility of individuals take over.

Both men are making a case that America is set apart—in a good way—from the rest of the world. Obama's view is that the goodness of America comes from a willingness to make shared sacrifices for the common good—often through the vehicle of government. Romney believes that America's exceptionalism is born of singular struggle and success. They are two sides of a similar, if not the same, coin.

But both messages speak to the big argument that 2012 will turn on: What does it mean to be American? Is it different, in a posteconomic collapse, post-9/11 world, than it was fifteen years ago? Are we still the dominant superpower in the world? Should we be? How long will we be? And if we aren't—or won't be at some time in the foreseeable future—what does that tell us about who we are?

Anxiety about our collective future reigns. Obama and Romney have to find ways to soothe that anxiety. Whoever does that better is likely to win in November.

# ACKNOWLEDGMENTS

Writing your first book is like jumping off a cliff into the water below. Even if you want to do it, you need a push to get you underway. Sean Desmond, my editor at Crown, spent years nudging me ever so gently toward the edge. Charlie Cook, John Harris, Tim Curran, Jim Brady, Russ Walker, Paul Volpe, and Marcus Brauchli all did their part—each in his own way—preparing me for the jump. So did Dan Balz and Jon Cohen, both of the *Washington Post;* and Chuck Todd, Andrea Mitchell, Brooke Brower, and John Bailey, all of NBC, who helped me with research. When I decided it was time, the ever-patient Gail Ross and Howard Yoon at the Ross-Yoon Agency walked me through the final preparations. I could never have imagined leaping without the three people who have helped make The Fix what it is today: Aaron Blake, Rachel Weiner, and Felicia Sonmez. I would never have had the chance to think about doing this without the opportunities my parents—John and Maryellen—made sure I got. And, anyone who has met me knows that I don't take a step without the love and support of my wife, Gia, and my son, Charlie. Thanks to all of you. I took the plunge.

# ABOUT THE AUTHOR

Chris Cillizza writes The Fix, a politics blog for the *Washington Post*. He also serves as managing editor of Postpolitics.com, the online home for the organization's political coverage. Chris is an MSNBC political analyst and regularly appears on NPR's *Diane Rehm Show*. He's passionate about three things: politics, Catholic University field hockey (his wife is the head coach), and Georgetown University basketball (he is an alum). He lives in Virginia with his wife and children.